Preparing a DUI Defense

A Practical Guide for Defending DUI Cases

John Ingrassia and Kathleen V. Wells

ASPATORE

Inside the Minds Project Manager, Caitlin Keiper edited by Eddie Fournier; proofread by Melanie Zimmerman

For additional copies or customer service inquiries, please e-mail west.customer.service@thomson.com.

ISBN 978-0-314-27891-3

Mat #41219195

ASPATORE

Aspatore Books, a Thomson Reuters business, exclusively publishes C-Level executives and partners from the world's most respected companies and law firms. Each publication provides professionals of all levels with proven business and legal intelligence from industry insiders—direct and unfiltered insight from those who know it best. Aspatore Books is committed to publishing an innovative line of business and legal titles that lay forth principles and offer insights that can have a direct financial impact on the reader's business objectives.

Dedication and Acknowledgements

I would like to thank my legal assistant Susan Bennett for her valuable time and assistance provided in typing and proofreading this book.

In addition, my thanks also go to my legal assistant Pattie Stellwag and my lawfirm's information and technology director Peter Warth. Both Pattie and Peter provided valuable assistance in meeting deadlines for this book, for which I am truly greatful.

This book would not have been a possibility without my co-author, associate, and friend Kathleen Wells Esq. Kathleen has been working at my side for more than ten and half years and counting. Simply put, she is the best appellate attorney with whom I have ever had the privilege of working. Her skills as an attorney are only surpassed by her qualities as a person.

I also wish to thank my parents, the Hon. Angelo and Judith Ingrassia. Through their guidance and love, both my mother and father instilled in me at a very young age to always do my best and that success does not come without hard work. Each day I strive to follow their values and I owe my parents a debt that I will never truly be able to repay.

I also want to thank my two daughters, Shelby and Chloe, for their unconditional love and support. Although I may not be home at dinnertime every night and I may occassionaly have a work commitment to cause me to be late for a cheerleading, swimming, or softball event, my love for the two of you has no limits.

Finally, to my wife, Annette Ingrassia, for whom my love also has no limits. Without her, this book would only have been a thought in my imagination. She is the foundation of our family and through her encouragement and support, that simple thought in my imagination has become a reality. Thank you for your love, your support, and for showing me how to believe in myself.

CONTENTS

Introduction

Although this book has been physically in the making for the past twelve months, in reality, it has been a work in progress for the past eighteen years of defending citizens accused of driving under the influence of alcohol (DUI). We actually decided to write this book to help fellow attorneys. By drawing from our experiences and lessons learned over the years, we are hopeful that through this book, attorneys, young and experienced alike, who take on defending a DUI case may better serve their clients and their profession as a whole.

DUI is a serious act and can have tragic and devastating consequences. Nevertheless, there are constitutional protections that apply to every person accused of a crime and such protections do not disappear in DUI cases. DUI is virutally the only crime where a person can be convicted based upon another person's opinion. Breath alcohol test devices are routinely accepted as accurate and reliable based on certain averages and assumptions. Penalties for DUI have become more and more severe over recent years, which require all defense practitioners to be ever more vigilant and prepared when deciding to defend a client accused of DUI.

We are hopeful that the materials contained in the book will be helpful to all of our brother and sister criminal defense attorneys who are called upon to defend a person accused of DUI.

Notes to Readers

Throughout this book, DUI is used as the collective term to describe any driving under the influence or driving while intoxicated (DWI) charge. In instances where the text refers to New York State law, DWI is used.

Additionally, DUI/DWI cases are handled according to individual state laws. We practice in New York, and therefore have used examples from New York State law throughout the book to clarify our points. Although much of the practical advice may be the same from state-to-state, each practitioner should check the specific rules of his/her state when defending a client in a DUI case.

1

The Initial Client Interview

When an individual accused of driving while under the influence of alcohol (DUI) comes into your office, the initial client interview is one of the most significant aspects of the case. It is the best opportunity for the attorney to get a detailed explanation of the arrest as well as the details leading up to the arrest.

Ascertaining the details of the client's activities leading up to the arrest is significant, because often DUI cases are defended using a defense that your client's blood-alcohol content was not what the test results report it to be. By obtaining the specific details of the client's activities leading up to the arrest, you are able to ascertain what alcoholic beverages your client was consuming and when they were consuming the drinks. Frequently, the police officer only asks what and how much your client had to drink. They do not inquire as to when your client first or last consumed the alcoholic beverage in relation to the time your client operated the vehicle. In addition to determining what type of alcoholic consumption took place, you also need to determine whether your client was engaged in any type of activities that may have exposed the client to any substances that could be reported as ethanol in a breath test. These would include individuals being exposed to solvents, paint thinners, mouthwash, and other types of chemicals.

You also want the initial interview to include asking what your client's typical drinking habits are, and, for example, finding out if your client was arrested after driving from home. If your client is accused of drinking at home, you want to determine how much alcohol is typically kept in their home.

Gathering Names of Potential Witnesses

The initial interview is also the first opportunity to gain information regarding any potential witnesses who were present with your client earlier during the day, during the period of time when the client is alleged to have consumed alcoholic beverages as well as at the time of the stop and arrest. In certain situations, an effective defense can be established by building a timeline setting forth what your client was doing and whom he or she was with in the hours leading up to the operation of the motor vehicle and the stop by police. It is a good idea to use a private investigator to interview witnesses to obtain favorable statements. A private investigator should be used to interview witnesses as opposed to the attorney conducting the initial interview to avoid any potential conflicts of interest resulting in the attorney who conducted the interview possibly becoming a witness in the case, should the witness interviewed ultimately change his or her story.

Another important aspect of the initial client interview is to obtain from the client, or any other witnesses, the precise location of the stop as well as the location where any field sobriety testing was done so that photographs and/or video can be taken to establish any potential defects in the surface where the sobriety testing was done. It is also helpful for the attorney to go to the location of the traffic stop and check it out. This will enable the attorney to have a better sense of the topography, geography, directions of nearby traffic, and so on so the attorney will be better equipped to cross-examine the police officer about these things.

The Client's Information

The initial client interview also provides the opportunity for you to get vital information regarding your client. Several areas of information are essential to have in order to adequately defend your client on a DUI charge. These areas include any type of physical or mental health issues your client has that can be used in attempting to effectuate a favorable plea bargain or in defending the case through litigation. In addition, your client's employment background is significant for such reasons as whether his or her employment causes him or her to be exposed to any type of chemicals or any other substances that could artificially inflate breath test results. Also, it is essential to know what your client does for a living, because DUI in many jurisdictions is a misdemeanor (criminal conviction) that could potentially have collateral consequences on their employment.

During the initial interview, the attorney also wants to find out as much as possible regarding the client's educational background, prior criminal history, any military service, as well as any community service organizations in which the client has participated. Once again, this information can be useful in helping to negotiate a favorable resolution for the client.

Fees

It is essential for the attorney to discuss all of the fees associated with defending a client charged with DUI. This must take place in the initial client interview. Some states require written retainer agreements to be executed by the client. Even if not required, the best practice is to have a written retainer agreement executed by the client and the attorney. The retainer agreement should set forth all of the fees associated with the representation as well as what the fee covers and does not cover. A copy of a sample retainer agreement is attached as Appendix A.

The Charges and Penalties Associated with Each Charge

At the initial client interview, the attorney should explain all of the charges, including different theories the prosecution may allege relating to driving under the influence of alcohol. Additionally, the attorney should set forth all of the potential penalties for each charge, including any mandatory fines and any other potential penalties, including incarceration, probation, license suspension/revocation, ignition interlock devices, and any associated collateral consequences or costs associated with a DUI conviction. These costs and collateral consequences can include Department of Motor Vehicles driver responsibility penalties, potential loss of insurance coverage, increased vehicle insurance premiums, loss of commercial driver's license, loss of employment and/or career-potential licenses or certifications, travel restrictions to enter other countries (like Canada), and Department of Motor Vehicles or court-mandated alcohol counseling and proof of successful rehabilitation.

In our experience, these items are best addressed up front in the initial interview so the prospective client has as complete an understanding as possible of the direct and collateral consequences a DUI arrest and potential conviction may carry. Also, being advised of this information early on will enable the client to best prepare his or her life, should these consequences be imposed in the future.

Addressing the Client's Alcohol Use and Options for Treatment

The initial client interview also provides the practitioner with the opportunity to address the client's alcohol use and options for treatment. Early in the case, it may be the client's choice whether he or she seeks treatment. However, at some point the court may mandate it. New York State now requires that a mandatory alcohol screening/assessment be done for all individuals charged with DWI who have a blood-alcohol content of 0.08 or above. Such assessment must take place either after arraignment or prior to imposition of sentence. NY VEH & TRAF § 1198-a.

An Overview of the Case

Finally, the initial client interview should involve an explanation from the attorney as to how the case proceeds from arraignment and thereon until the ultimate conclusion of the case. Although it is often not possible for the attorney to predict what the outcome of the case will be, the attorney must nevertheless give the client an overview of how the process works, including a potential estimate of how long the case may last. Most often, the atorney will only be able to provide estimates because the length of time it takes to resolve a case varies on a case-by-case basis that depends on a variety of factors.

The above is not an exhaustive list of everything that should be covered during the initial client interview, but rather a guideline to cover a variety of significant aspects of the case that should be addressed at the first client meeting.

2

The Arraignment

The arraignment is a first appearance in court when the court acquires personal jurisdiction over the defendant. The purpose of the arraignment is to advise the defendant of the charges against him or her and to make sure the defendant is aware of his or her rights with regard to those allegations.

The Initial Plea

At the arraignment, the judge will ask the defendant how he or she pleads. The plea can be either not guilty or guilty. Assuming the plea is not guilty, the court will typically set a schedule for discovery and motion practice. In New York State, the timeframe in which to demand discovery and file motions are established by statute. NY CRIM PRO §§ 100.45(4), 170.30(2), 200.95, 240.80, 240.90, 255.20. New York State also has temporary license suspension issues that may occur at the arraignment.

Suspension Due to Excessive Blood-Alcohol Test Result

In New York State, an individual who is alleged to have had a blood-alcohol content of 0.08 of 1 percent or more by weight as shown by chemical analysis of his or her blood, breath, urine, or saliva will have his or her license suspended temporarily upon arraignment by the court, provided that the court has a legally sufficient accusatory instrument charging the defendant with DWI and there is an original proper certification of the chemical test result. *See* NY VEH & TRAF §1193(2)(e)(7); *Pringle* v. *Wolfe*, 88 N.Y.2d 426 (1996). If the court finds that those elements are present, the licensee may present evidence that tends to rebut any of those initial findings. If the licensee is not successful in doing such, the court must mandatorily suspend the driver's license pending prosecution. The defendant is potentially eligible at that time for a hardship privilege issued by the court. After the first thirty days of the suspension, the defendant is potentially eligible for a pre-conviction conditional license issued by the Department of Motor Vehicles. NY VEH & TRAF § 1196(7). Significantly, if the court suspends your client's driver's license under this provision of law, he or she is not allowed to drive home from court, and therefore it is important to notify the client prior to court that he or she should make alternate arrangements for transportation home.

Temporary Suspension of a Driver's License Due to an Alleged Chemical Test Refusal

Many states require the court at the arraignment to suspend the operator's driver's license if there is an alleged refusal to submit to a chemical test. NY VEH & TRAF § 1194(2)(b). With this type of suspension, there is a temporary suspension that is imposed due to the alleged chemical test refusal, and in New York State, the licensee will then be entitled to a hearing before the Department of Motor Vehicles within fifteen days of the court's temporary suspension in order for a Department of Motor Vehicles administrative law judge to determine whether the alleged refusal will be sustained, thereby resulting in a one-year revocation of the defendant's driver's license. Notably, in New York State, if the court suspends due to a chemical test refusal, the individual is not eligible for any type of hardship privilege or conditional license at the time suspension is imposed.

Court-Ordered Alcohol Assessments and Screenings

In New York State, upon arraignment the court is required to order either an alcohol screening or assessment for any individual who is accused of committing DWI with a blood-alcohol content of 0.08 of 1 percent or more.

Mandatory screening involves the use of a standardized written screening instrument developed by the Office of Alcoholism and Substance Abuse Services to assess a defendant, to be administered by an alcohol or substance abuse professional. NY VEH & TRAF §§ 1198-a(2)(a) and (b).

Upon the arraignment of (or, at the discretion of the court, prior to sentencing) first-time violators charged with DWAI by drugs, DWAI by alcohol, aggravated DWI with a child, DWI common law, or DWI per se, and who either had a breath test result of less than 0.15 or refused the chemical test, must be screened by a treatment professional using a standardized written screening test. If the screening indicates that the person is abusing or dependant upon alcohol or drugs, he or she must undergo the mandatory assessment as set forth below. NY VEH & TRAF § 1198-a(2)(a).

A mandatory assessment is a court-ordered formal alcohol or substance abuse and dependency assessment by an alcohol or substance abuse professional or a licensed agency. NY VEH & TRAF § 1198-a(2)(b). Mandatory assessment is required under the following circumstances:

1. The screening process set forth above indicates abuse or dependence upon alcohol or drugs.
2. There is a charge of DWI or DWI per se and the blood-alcohol content was 0.15 or greater.
3. There is a charge of aggravated DWI per se.
4. One has been charged with violating any provision of NY VEH & TRAF § 1192 and has either (a) a prior conviction within the last five years for any provision of NY VEH & TRAF § 1192 or any of the Penal Law offenses that have as a necessary element a violation of NY VEH & TRAF § 1192 (such as vehicular assault or vehicular manslaughter), or (b) two or more such convictions within the preceding ten years. NY VEH & TRAF § 1198-a(2)(b).

The assessment shall be performed by an alcohol or substance abuse professional or a licensed agency that shall forward the results, in writing, to the court and to the defendant or his or her counsel within thirty days of the date of such order. NY VEH & TRAF § 1198-a(2)(c).

The chief administrator of the Office of Court Administration shall make available to all criminal courts in New York State a list of alcohol and substance abuse professionals and licensed agencies as provided by the Office of Alcoholism and Substance Abuse Services. NY VEH & TRAF § 1198-a(5).

When a sentence of probation or a conditional discharge is imposed upon a person who has been required to undergo an alcohol or substance abuse and dependency assessment, and such assessment indicates that such person is in need of treatment for alcohol or substance abuse or dependency, the court shall require, as a condition of such sentence, that such person participate in and successfully complete such treatment. Such treatment shall be provided by an alcohol or substance abuse professional or a licenced agency. NY VEH & TRAF § 1198-a(3).

In any case where the original charge was DWI per se, DWI common law, DWAI by drugs, or DWAI by combined influence of drugs or alcohol and any drug, and the court has accepted a plea to DWAI by alcohol (NY VEH & TRAF § 1192(1)), and such plea requires that the defendant attend and complete the Alcohol and Drug Rehabilitation Program (Drunk Driving Program, also known as DDP), including any assessment and treatment required thereby, the successful completion of the program shall be deemed to be in compliance with the provisions of NY VEH & TRAF § 1198-a.

Confidentiality of Records

The records and content of all screenings, assessments, and treatment conducted pursuant to NY VEH & TRAF § 1198-a, including the identity, diagnosis, and prognosis of each individual who is the subject of such records, and including any statements or admissions of such individual made during the course of such screenings, assessments, and treatment, shall be confidential, shall not be disclosed except as authorized by NY VEH & TRAF §§ 1198-a(6)(a) and (b)(i)(ii)(iii), and shall not be entered or received as evidence at any civil, criminal, or administrative trial, hearing, or proceeding. No person, other than a defendant to whom such records are disclosed, may redisclose such records.

Such records may only be disclosed as follows:

1. To a court for the sole purpose of requiring a defendant charged with or convicted of a violation of NY VEH & TRAF §§1192 (1), (2), (2-a), (3), (4), or (4-a) to undergo alcohol or substance abuse or dependency assessment or treatment
2. To the defendant or his or her authorized representative
3. To medical personnel to the extent necessary to meet a bona fide medical emergency

NY VEH & TRAF §§ 1198-a(6)(a) and (b)(i)(ii)(iii).

Bail Issues

Arraignment is also the first opportunity for the court to address the issue of bail pending the next court date. The overall purpose of bail is to secure the defendant's appearance at each successive court date. In New York State, for example, the court must consider a variety of factors in determining whether to set bail. NY CRIM PRO § 510.30. The attorney should always ask for the court to release the client on his or her own recognizance, and if the court is reluctant to do so, you can ask the court to attach certain conditions to that release on recognizance. These conditions could be that the defendant obtain alcohol treatment, not operate a motor vehicle, refrain from consuming alcoholic beverages, and/or report to a probation officer during the pendency of the case.

If the court determines that bail should be set, the attorney should ask that the court set bail in either a cash or bond alternative to give the client and his or her family the best available means to secure the client's release from jail during the pendency of the case.

How the Client Should Dress

We only get one chance to make a first impression. It is important for the practitioner to remember that the first time the client appears in court for arraignment will be the first time the judge and prosecutor see the client with regard to the charge. As such, it is imperative that your client make a good impression with the court and the prosecutor. Having the client dress in appropriate clothing is an important detail not to overlook in order to have your client make the best possible impression on the court and the prosecutor. While the manner of your client's appearance may not provide a factual or legal defense to the case, it may ultimately be useful in negotiating a favorable plea bargain disposition, because the court and prosecutor will have the sense that the defendant has shown respect for the court and for the seriousness of the matter.

3

Discovery Demands

In defending a DUI case, it is imperative to make detailed discovery demands to assist in the defense of the case. The discovery demands should include demands for information relating to the stopping of your client's vehicle, your client's performance on field sobriety tests, and all aspects of the chemical test, including the timing of the test, the results of the test, any breath tests that were run, a copy of the maintenance history of the chemical test device, calibrations and any certifications of the component parts of the breath test device, and certifications as to the qualifications of the operator of the test.

Examining Your State's Discovery Statute to Ascertain What You Are Entitled To

To thoroughly frame your discovery demands, it is imperative to examine your state's discovery statute to see what a defendant is entitled to receive upon a demand to produce. You should track your discovery statutes to make those specific demands, and then further expand your demands by demanding anything further that your specific case requires. A sample discovery demand is attached as Appendix B.

Demand for Brady Material

Both New York State and federal law require the prosecution to turn over evidence/materials possessed or controlled by or known to any law enforcement personnel that is exculpatory or otherwise can be used for impeachment of the witnesses.

Under the federal constitutional standard, disclosure of information and evidence in favor of the accused is required when disclosure would create a reasonable probability of acquittal of the charged offense. *See generally Youngblood v. West Virginia*, 547 US 867 (2006). When, however, a defendant has made a specific request for favorable information, disclosure is also necessary under a state constitutional materiality standard when there is a reasonable possibility that it would affect the verdict on any charged offense. *See People v. Vilardi*, 76 NY2d 67 (1990).

Notably, both the US Supreme Court and the New York State Court of Appeals have held that there is no distinction between material that is exculpatory and material that qualifies as impeachment material. As such, the prosecutor's duty is not in any way diminished, because the "Brady material" only affects the credibility of a prosecution witness. *See United States v. Bagley*, 473 US 667 (1985); *Giglio v. United States*, 405 US 150 (1972); *People v. Fuentes*, 12 NY3d 259 (2009).

Demanding Videotapes of the Arrest and Booking Room and Breath Test

Many police departments now have video recordings of the arrest/booking room as well as the location where the breath test is actually administered. A detailed demand for the production of any videotapes relating to the scene of the arrest, as well as the booking rooms and breath test, should be made. This is significant because many patrol cars now have videotapes of a subject's driving and of the stop. In addition, sobriety testing may be captured on videotape as well as audiotape.

Obtaining booking room videotapes as well as any videotapes of the breath test is significant, because it will further show your client's condition as he or she appears in the booking room. Moreover, frequently you can establish breaches in the mandatory observation period to establish that your client was not continuously observed prior to the administration of the breath test. These videotapes are discoverable regardless of whether the prosecution intends to introduce them at trial, and there can be sanctions imposed for the failure to preserve and/or provide such tapes.

Noncompliance with Discovery Demands: What to Do and When to Do It

In determining what to do in the event of noncompliance with discovery demands, you need to determine what the most probable outcome will be. The court does have several remedies, which can include a dismissal of the charges. That is a very unusual remedy due to its drastic nature. The court may also impose adverse inferences against the prosecution for failing to produce and preserve such evidence, or it can preclude the admissibility of the same.

Sample Discovery Demands

A sample demand to produce is attached as Appendix B.

4

Motion Practice

Typically, counsel will need to file a motion to suppress physical evidence consisting of the chemical test results as well as a motion to suppress any type of admissions or confessions of the defendant. In addition, you will want to consider filing motions to preclude the use of prior convictions, particularly prior convictions for DUI-related offenses, if your client is to take the stand. A sample DWI motion is included as Appendix C.

Reasons for Filing a Motion to Suppress

A reason why a motion to suppress evidence should be filed is because every individual accused of a crime has a right to suppress evidence obtained by law enforcement or their agents due to alleged constitutional infirmities. In a DUI case, this includes challenging the basis for the initial stop of the client as well as whether the police had reasonable cause to believe the client had operated a motor vehicle while under the influence of alcohol, thereby giving them the authority to arrest the operator and ask the operator to submit to a chemical test.

Basis to Stop Subject's Motor Vehicle

The police stopping a motor vehicle constitutes a seizure of the driver and all occupants therein, and it therefore requires that the police have a lawful basis to do so. In New York State, police must have a reasonable suspicion to believe that a violation or crime has been committed in order for the vehicle to be stopped. *See People v. Ingle*, 36 NY2d 413 (1975); *cf. People v. Robinson*, 97 NY2d 341 (2001). In *Robinson*, the New York Court of Appeals affirmed the validity of a pretext stop provided that there was probable cause that a driver has committed a traffic violation. *See Robinson* 97 NY2d at 350.

Litigating the Basis for the Stop at the Suppression Hearing

In the vast majority of DUI suppression hearings, the courts will find that the police had a lawful basis to stop the subject's vehicle. Notwithstanding this tendency, it is very important for the defense attorney to thoroughly review the statutes relating to the charge on which the officer is basing the stop.

The following are just a few examples of cases that were successfully defended because the basis for the stop was challenged:

1. Police officer charges client with failing to signal when pulling out of a private parking lot. This is not a violation of a law. *See Byer v. Jackson*, 241 A.D.2d 943 (4th Dept. 1997).
2. Police stop of subject's vehicle for having inadequate reverse lights due to only one light functioning. NY VEH & TRAF § 375(2)(a)(34) only requires one reverse light to be functioning.
3. Police officer stops vehicle for crossing over hazardous marking due to driver crossing white fog line on right side of the road. Crossing white fog line does not constitute a violation of the Vehicle and Traffic Law, as crossing the line is not prohibited but merely discouraged. *See People v. Shulman*, 836 N.Y.S.2d 488 (2006).
4. Inadequate rear license plate lamp in violation of NY VEH & TRAF § 372.2(a)(4), which requires light to illuminate rear plate for at least fifty feet. Therefore, the police officer must articulate at the suppression hearing that the license plate was not illuminated from within that certain required distance.

Challenging Civilian Informants

DUI cases sometimes present a fact pattern where the police stop a motorist based upon a civilian complaint. If this happens, you must challenge the stop on the ground that the civilian informant did not have a valid basis of knowledge to impart the information or that the informant was not reliable. These cases can be effectively defended, particularly where the only basis for the officer having stopped your client's vehicle is based upon the information provided by the civilian informant. That is, the officer does not observe any independent violation of law that would afford him or her the right to stop the motorist. When an officer makes a stop based upon a civilian informant, the information constitutes hearsay and sometimes even double or triple hearsay. Typically, this happens by a call coming into the police station by the civilian informant reporting a possibly intoxicated driver. Thereafter, the dispatcher radios to the police officer the information that was provided by the civilian informant. Sometimes a triple hearsay situation develops where the civilian informant makes a 911 call and then the 911 center provides the information to the local police department's dispatcher who then radios the information to the officer who makes the stop. Many times, the source of the information turns out to be an anonymous call in that the police department does not obtain the name of the person who is providing the information. In *People v. Havelka*, 45 NY2d 636 (1978) the New York Court of Appeals made clear that even if the police communication provides *prima facie* support for the police action, it nevertheless becomes a requirement that the people produce the sender of the information at the suppression hearing. The district attorney seldomly will subpoena the civilian informant at the suppression hearing, and if that informant is anonymous, the prosecution will not be able to establish their burden at the suppression hearing upon a motion to suppress that properly challenges the source of the information.

Roadblocks

In a case involving a DWI sobriety checkpoint, a successful challenge can be made when the people fail to present evidence of a lawful purpose of the checkpoint and of a constitutionally permissible policy for conducting stops at the checkpoint. *See In Re Muhammad F.*, 94 NY2d 136 (1999), cert.denied sub non, *New York v. Boswell*, 531 US 1044 (2000); *see also People v. Scott*, 63 NY2d 518 (1984). Many times at the suppression hearing, the prosecutor will fail to establish whether any policies were in effect detailing how the sobriety checkpoint would be effectuated. Once again, DUI sobriety checkpoints have passed constitutional muster provided the discretion of the officers who are running the sobriety checkpoint is limited. Counsel for the accused should always make a detailed demand to produce for any written policies and procedures regarding the DUI sobriety checkpoint that was employed in the given case.

Posting

The US Department of Transportation's *Federal Highway Administration Manual on Uniform Traffic Control Devices for Streets and Highways* was adopted by New York State on September 13, 2007. This manual controls where traffic control device signs have to be placed. When litigating cases at suppression hearings and at trial, if the police officer fails to testify as to any posting of the traffic control device signs, an application should be made at the conclusion of the hearing and/or trial that the prosecution failed to meet its burden in establishing their standard of proof due to the insufficient evidence with regard to posting. *See, e.g., People v. Brahms*, 746 N.Y.S.2d 529(2002) (holding that properly posted no left turn signs must exist in order to sustain conviction for disobeying a traffic control device).

Right to Counsel Issues

In addition, counsel should consider inquiring whether there was any right to counsel violation regarding a defendant's request to speak to an attorney prior to submitting to a chemical test.

In New York State, an individual has a qualified right to consult with an attorney to determine whether to submit to a chemical test provided that the request does not unreasonably interfere with the matter at hand. *See People v. Gursey*, 22 NY2d 224 (1968).

What Is Required to File a Motion to Suppress Evidence

Under New York State Criminal Procedure Law, a motion to suppress evidence must be filed in writing and on notice to the prosecution. The motion must contain sufficient sworn allegations of fact establishing the alleged unlawful conduct by the police. Notably, an affidavit of the defendant is not required, as the motion may be based upon information and belief provided that the source of such information and grounds for such belief are set forth in the attorney's affirmation. NY CRIM PRO § 710.60(1).

5

The Suppression Hearing

The burden of proof at a suppression hearing is initially upon the prosecution. As such, the prosecution initially bears the burden of moving forward to establish the legality of the police conduct in the first instance. Once the people have done so, the burden shifts to the defense to somehow establish that the police conduct was constitutionally invalid. Ways to establish that include attacking police conduct. As described in the previous chapter, this can be done by probing the police officer with questions relative to the initial stopping of the vehicle, as well as attempting to establish that the officer lacked reasonable cause to believe the defendant was under the influence of alcohol even if the stop is valid. In Chapter 8, there will be much more detailed discussions and examples of how to cross-examine the arresting officer relative to a variety of issues relating to the DUI stop and arrest. Those areas of cross-examination discussed in Chapter 8 are equally applicable to challenging the lawfulness of the stop and arrest at a suppression hearing.

After the prosecution has presented its case at the suppression hearing, the defendant, if he or she so desires, may present evidence to rebut the prosecution's case.

Defendant's Right to Testify at a Suppression Hearing

In the event that the defendant does testify at the suppression hearing, the defendant will be subjected to cross-examination and such cross-examination may be later used at trial to impeach the defendant in the event that the defendant testifies at trial. In addition, the defendant has the right to present other relevant evidence in the form of testimony of other witnesses or other documentary evidence.

Sample Cross-Examinations

A sample cross-examination from a suppression hearing can be found as Appendix D.

6

The Trial

In New York State, an individual charged with DWI is entitled to a jury trial provided the individual is nineteen years of age or above at the time of the commission of the alleged crime. That right to a jury trial, however, can be waived and there are certain situations where an individual may want to consider waiving a jury depending upon the issues involved as well as the judge presiding over the case.

One may want to consider waiving a jury if the case involves a purely legal defense as opposed to a factual defense, such as when a client was not actually operating the motor vehicle on a public highway as that term is defined under your specific state law.

Strategies for Jury Selection

The defense of a DUI case has become increasingly more difficult over the past decade. Harsher laws, increased law enforcement, and public sensitivity to this subject have all contributed to this result.

The process of jury selection is an opportunity to help level the playing field in the defense of a DUI case and educate the jury to try to give your client a better chance of successfully defending a DUI charge.

The defense of any type of DUI case is very difficult given the public's dislike for the crime of DUI. To help your chances of successfully defending the charge, the jury has to be educated that DUI is the only crime a person can be convicted of based upon another individual's opinion as opposed to actual fact. Put another way, when a jury returns a guilty verdict at least as to common law DUI, they are accepting, beyond a reasonable doubt, the police officer's opinion as to a defendant's condition. Although the opinion must be supported by facts observed by the officer, it is necessary to focus the jury's attention on the ultimate fact that in order to be found guilty your client must be convicted based upon a person's opinion.

Along this theme, jury selection provides a wonderful opportunity to use examples of when all of us in our own individual experiences have formed an opinion about something that turned out to be wrong.

When it is ultimately time to give your summation to the jury, jurors can be reminded of these issues raised during jury selection. The difference between fact and opinion allows you to argue to the jury that by returning a not guilty verdict it does not mean the jurors found that the officer was lying, but rather that his or her opinion was wrong or mistaken. That is, the officer misinterpreted what he or she observed.

Dealing with Opinion Testimony and Educating the Jury about the Difference Between Subjective and Objective Opinions

It is extremely important to highlight to the jury the difference between an individual's objective opinion and subjective opinion. Often when I am litigating a DUI case, I will inquire of several members of the jury what their interests are. Once I learn what an individual juror's interests are, I will begin to question that juror about his or her understanding of the difference between a subjective fact and an objective fact. People assess things objectively and subjectively every day to form opinions about a given set of circumstances. For example, if a prospective juror indicates that he or she is a baseball fan, I almost always pose questions about baseball players. I will make a statement that Willie Mays is the greatest center fielder in the history of major league baseball. I will then follow that up with a question of whether anybody disagrees with the opinion. Thereafter, I begin to explain my reasons why I believe Willie Mays was the greatest center fielder of all time. Given that example, I get the jury to understand that my statement about Willie Mays is not an objective fact but is rather my subjective opinion. I then turn to the jury and advise them that other people may disagree with me, and some people may believe Mickey Mantle or Joe

Dimaggio was the greatest center fielder in the history of major league baseball. This type of questioning leaves powerful visual images to which you can refer during summation to help you argue for your client by simply arguing to the jury that the officer's opinion is his or her own subjective opinion. The jury must then be reminded that they must view those facts in an objective fashion so they are convinced beyond a reasonable doubt that in fact your client was intoxicated.

Other examples of distinguishing between a subjective opinion and objective fact is by holding up different color pens, one red and one black. I will ask an individual juror or the jury panel as a whole, while holding the black pen, whether the statement "This pen is black" is a fact or opinion. Unanimously the jury will all indicate that it is a fact that the pen is black. I will then make a subjective statement that the tie I am wearing is the nicest tie ever made. I will then ask an individual juror or the jury as a whole if that statement is an opinion or fact. Unanimously they will all agree that it is merely my own subjective opinion. These types of examples are virtually limitless, but their impact can have tremendous value in defending an individual charged with DUI.

Constitutional Safeguards

Jury selection also provides an excellent opportunity to reinforce all of the constitutionally guaranteed principles enjoyed by every criminal defendant. It is extremely important to emphasize to the jury that the defense has no burden of proof. Moreover, along with the burden of proof, a defendant in a criminal case has no obligation to testify. I will often explain to the jury that I could sit down next to my client right at that moment and not be heard from again and the jury cannot draw any type of negative inference from that. I explain to them that although it is not required, they will hear from me many more times before the end of the trial because the job of the defense attorney is to challenge, question, and probe the prosecution's evidence.

We often learn as young children that there are always two sides to every story. I remind the jury that a criminal trial is not the same as our common life experiences. I explain this to the jury because a jury does not get to hear the defendant's side of the story unless the defendant elects to testify on his or her own behalf. Again, this reinforces your client's right to remain silent. I will also advise the jury that if my client decides to testify, that does not change the burden of proof. That is, my client does not need to persuade you that he or she is telling the truth.

Nature of the DUI Charge

Upon selecting a jury on a DUI charge, counsel must be aware of the sensitive nature of DUI charges. No one condones DUI. That being the case, it is essential to enlighten the jury that while it is understandable that everyone is against operating a motor vehicle while under the influence of alcohol, it is not a crime to consume alcoholic beverages and then operate a motor vehicle. Rather, the Vehicle and Traffic Law only penalizes individuals who operate a motor vehicle while they are under the influence of alcohol as that is defined by the Vehicle and Traffic Law. I question the prospective panel as to the issue of whether anyone believes a person should not operate a motor vehicle after having had anything of an alcoholic nature to drink. If any of the jurors raise their hand in agreement with that statement (and usually this will be the case), I have the potential to challenge that juror for cause. If that occurs, you must question that juror regarding his or her willingness to follow the judge's instructions. If he or she still believes that anyone who consumes any amount of an alcoholic beverage should not operate a motor vehicle, you are in a position to successfully argue to the court that the juror has an unwillingness to follow the court's instruction and therefore should be challenged for cause.

A Police Officer's Testimony

A DUI case will always rely on the testimony of police witnesses. To effectively select a jury, you must get the jury to agree that a police officer's testimony is to be given no more weight than any other witness's testimony, including that of the defendant. An easy way to support this issue is by pointing out to the jury that the police officer can be mistaken as opposed to lying about facts. This is a very effective technique in the defense of any case, but in particular a DUI case. One effective way this idea can be brought out during jury selection is to ask prospective jurors to raise their hands if they have ever been given a speeding ticket. Often, several members of the panel will indicate that they have been given a ticket. I then follow up by asking whether anyone who has received a speeding ticket believed he or she was given the ticket unjustly, that is, was anyone given a ticket for speeding who believed he or she in fact was not speeding. Once again, very frequently, one or more individuals will raise their hand. This concept flows nicely when those individuals who were given tickets were claimed to have been clocked by some type of radar device. By questioning the jurors in this regard, you can expose to the entire panel that individuals on the jury panel have taken issue with the results of a radar speeding ticket that can show the inaccuracy or unreliability of machines. This builds a logical bridge to attack the chemical breath test result as being unreliable, just as the radar device was.

Field Sobriety Testing

In DUI cases, there will typically be sobriety test evidence submitted by the prosecution. The fact of the matter is that many jurors have no experience with field sobriety testing. A simple way to attack field sobriety tests is to inquire of the jurors whether they have ever had difficulty doing any type of tests that require coordination. Many times, there are people who are simply non-athletic and will readily admit to having difficulty performing simple coordination tasks. I like to use the example of a trained Olympic athlete, perhaps a gymnast or ice skater who has trained and completed tens of thousands of hours in preparation for the Olympics. Ultimately, I give the example as to whether they have ever seen such an Olympian make a simple mistake, whether it's a gymnast on the balance beam or a skater on the ice. I like to use the analogy that people can react differently under a stressful or nervous type of setting. My experience is that every juror will concede that being pulled over by the police and being investigated for a DUI charge would certainly be a stressful experience. By using this type of example, you can loop that together with your summation to give the jurors an explanation of why your client did poorly on the sobriety tests.

Also, it can be very effective to ask jurors whether they had any difficulty with a sport when first learning the sport. For example, if there are any golfers on the panel, you can ask them whether they had difficulty hitting a golf ball the first time they played golf. You can then ask them if they improved with practice. Almost always, people do. Remind the jurors that your client did not get the chance to practice the field sobriety tests.

Breath Test Machines

If your case involves a breath test, I like to briefly *voir dire* the jury panel as to their understanding of breath test devices and whether they have heard anything about them that led them to form opinions about them. Inherent with any type of chemical breath test device is a built-in margin of error plus or minus 0.01 of 1 percent. That is, if a chemical test result is a 0.10, most officers will readily admit that, assuming everything is working perfectly and the test was administered in proper fashion, the most the officer can tell you is that the subject's blood alcohol was 0.10, 0.11, or 0.09. There is a 20 percent difference between those three results. You can then use everyday experiences to question the jurors as to whether they believe a potential 20 percent swing is something with which they feel comfortable. For example, you can ask jurors if their doctor prescribed a certain medication for them or their children and advised that the medication may result in serious side effects such as paralysis or kidney failure or stroke in 20 percent of the patients who use that medication, whether anybody on that panel would be willing to take that medication or administer it to their children.

Another way to emphasize the point is to ask the jury if they would accept all-expenses-paid plane tickets to Hawaii if they knew the airplane had a 20 percent chance of having engine failure in midair. By looping these themes into the reliability of the breath test result, you will be able to condition the jury, and then when you go back before the jury during your summation, you can attack the breath test result to establish reasonable doubt.

These types of questions can be very effective in the DUI case where you have a low chemical test result or even where you have a high chemical test result and the prosecution's common law evidence is weak.

Refusal Cases

Selecting a jury in a refusal case is a challenging job. Clients who refuse to take a chemical test often receive a devastating jury instruction. It is incumbent on defense counsel to enlighten the jury of reasons (other than fear of the test result) why a person may refuse a chemical test.

Initially, it is a good idea to begin by educating a jury that a person has the right to refuse a chemical test. In addition, it is quite common for people to have heard that breath test devices are not reliable, and thus because they have heard this, they opt to refuse. Sometimes people refuse because they use medications that are made of alcohol and are afraid the medications will register as though they had been drinking alcohol. Ultimately, during summation you will have to address why your client refused, and that task must start during jury selection.

The above thoughts are merely some recommendations and are not intended in any way to be exhaustive of the areas the practitioner should cover during jury selection. Some courts impose time restrictions during jury selection, so you must target the specific areas you feel are most important to cover. Once again, due to the unique nature of DUI charges, it is also important to flush out through the prospective jurors their personal opinions as to alcohol consumption as well as whether any individuals are members of Mothers Against Drunk Driving or Students Against Destructive Decisions or any other anti-drunk driving groups. In addition, it is vital to inquire whether they or anyone they know has ever been a victim of a drunk driving-related accident.

Peremptory Juror Challenges and for Cause Juror Challenges

In selecting a jury in a DUI case, you must familiarize yourself with your state's law regarding how many peremptory challenges you get. For example, in New York State for a misdemeanor DWI, you are entitled to three peremptory challenges, and for a felony, you are entitled to ten peremptory challenges. A peremptory challenge is a challenge to which you are not attaching any specific reason, and you exercise that by dismissing a prospective juror.

The other type of challenge is a challenge for cause. A challenge for cause deals with some type of bias/prejudice a prospective juror has that will prevent the defendant or the prosecution from receiving a fair trial. These challenges are unlimited.

Sample Jury Selection Questions

This line of questioning is relevant to trying to get a juror to understand that there is a difference between somebody's subjective opinion and an objective fact. In a DUI case, you must educate the jury that the district attorney will be asking you to return a guilty verdict based upon an officer's subjective opinion of your client's condition. The following scenario is illustrative of how people's subjective opinions can differ from objective facts.

> *Question by attorney to prospective juror #1:* Do you listen to music?
>
> *Answer by prospective juror #1:* Yes.
>
> *Question by attorney to prospective juror #1:* What type of music is your favorite music?
>
> *Answer by prospective juror #1:* I like rock music.
>
> *Question by attorney to prospective juror #2:* Prospective juror #1 just indicated that rock music is her favorite type of music. Do you agree with the fact that rock music is the best type of music?
>
> *Answer by prospective juror #2:* No, I believe country music is the best type of music.

The above questions and answers illustrate how two people in the same setting can have different beliefs as to what the best type of music is. That is because it is their subjective opinion as to what type of music is the best. You can then expound on that example by breaking it down even further as to whom the greatest rock artist is and who the greatest country artist is. You will get many different opinions. The fact is that nobody is wrong under that scenario, but rather they are just holding on to their subjective opinions as to what is most pleasing to them. You then need to demonstrate to the jury that there is a difference between a subjective opinion and an objective fact. This can be done simply by holding a red or blue pen in your hand and asking a prospective juror what color those respective pens are. Once a juror answers correctly that it is a blue or red or any other color pen that it might be, you have now demonstrated to them that that is a fact and not an opinion. A DUI case is one of the only cases where an individual accused can be convicted based upon somebody's opinion as opposed to an established fact. By driving that point home during jury selection, you will be able to ultimately come back before the jury during your summation using those examples in attacking the reliability of the arresting officer's opinion that your client was intoxicated. Once again, the officer may not necessarily be lying, but rather may merely be mistaken as to his or her subjective opinion as to your client's condition.

Breath Test

It is also important to have questions posed to the prospective jurors regarding their understanding of how a breath test device works and whether they have heard anything about a breath test. Significantly, you can begin to establish early during jury selection that in life we do expect things to be 100 percent accurate and not have a margin of error of plus or minus 10 percent either way, as most breath test devices do. The following can be used to establish that:

> *Question by attorney to prospective juror:* Mr. X, when you file your tax return each year with the federal and state government, you are required to account for every dollar you earned, correct?
>
> *Answer by prospective juror:* Yes.
>
> *Question:* What would happen if you only accounted for 90 or 95 percent of the money you earned?
>
> *Answer:* That return would not be accurate, and I may be exposing myself to problems with the IRS.
>
> *Question:* That is because the government requires you to report things with 100 percent accuracy and account for 100 cents on every dollar you earn as opposed to 90 cents on every dollar you earn, correct?
>
> *Answer:* Correct, I have to account for 100 percent.

That line of questioning has now established that the government requires citizens to be 100 percent accurate, yet they can be 90 percent accurate as to the reliability of a breath test device when seeking to obtain a conviction against a fellow citizen accused.

Another example of attacking a breath test is by giving examples of the variance of temperature that is allowed for the simulator solution used in most breath test devices. In most breath test devices, a simulator solution containing a known quantity of ethyl alcohol must be kept at a certain constant temperature of 34 degrees centigrade plus or minus one-tenth of a degree. That is, the temperature must be 34.0, 34.1, or 33.9 degrees centigrade. You can then ask jurors whether they would be satisfied if there was that range for a margin of error relative to any type of medical diagnostic test they or a loved one were undergoing to determine whether they have a serious condition or disease that requires certain types of treatment depending upon the accuracy of the diagnosis. Most people in those situations would demand that the result would have to be 100 percent accurate with no margin of error.

During jury selection, you must try to be as imaginative as possible to think of the various issues that come up during a DUI trial to educate the jury to give your client the best possible chance to obtain an acquittal.

7

The Opening Statement

In New York State, a defendant has the right but is not required to make an opening statement in either a jury or non-jury trial. In a jury trial, you always want to make an opening statement because the prosecutor is required to make an opening statement. In a non-jury trial, if the prosecution agrees not to make an opening statement, you might not want to make an opening statement as well. You will need to know who your judge is and what his or her preferences are before you determine whether you wish to waive an opening statement in a non-jury trial.

The Purpose of an Opening Statement

The purpose of an opening statement is not only to give an overview of the case to the jury, but it is also a time to educate the jury as to what happened in the case, what did not happen, and what could have happened. Depending upon what your specific defense is with regard to the trial, your opening statement will need to be tailored to those aspects of the defense. The following is a brief example of an opening statement when you are challenging the results of a blood alcohol test result based upon a breath test device:

> Good morning ladies and gentlemen. You have just heard the prosecutor give you her rendition of what she believes the evidence will likely show. Well ladies and gentlemen, I'm here to tell you what the evidence will in fact show. The evidence will show that my client, Kathy Smith, had just finished a long day of work at the ABC Corporation where she works as an auditor. After work, she and two of

her colleagues stopped by a local establishment where she had two glasses of white wine over a period of two and a half hours. Through the testimony of her two friends, Jane Doe and Mary Jones, we will demonstrate that she only had two glasses over that period of time. This will also be demonstrated by a credit card receipt showing her to have purchased two glasses of wine on her American Express card. After that two and a half hour period of time had gone by, Kathy said good night to her work colleagues, walked to the parking lot, got into the car, and put the keys in the ignition. Kathy then started the car, and began driving out of the parking lot onto Main Street. After going onto Main Street, she took Main Street to Main Street Extension where she entered Highway 17. Highway 17 has a posted 55 miles per hour speed limit, and in a rush to get home, Kathy did exceed the speed limit by traveling 63 miles per hour. It was while she was traveling at 63 miles per hour that Trooper Long observed my client driving in excess of the posted speed limit.

Trooper Long followed Kathy's car for about three quarters of a mile, and during that period of time, the only vehicle and traffic violation he observed was her speeding in excess of the posted speed limit. At no time did he see any type of erratic operation. At no time did he indicate that she exercised any type of difficulty either in terms of the time or the manner in which she pulled over in esponse to his having activated his emergency overhead lights.

After being stopped by the police, Kathy produced a valid New York State driver's license, registration, and insurance card. You will hear from Trooper Long himself that my client retrieved and handed all of the required documents to him without any difficulty at all with her coordination. After those documents were retrieved, the trooper indicated to my client that he detected an odor of an alcoholic beverage on her breath and asked her if she had

had anything to drink. Having nothing to hide, Kathy told the trooper that she had had two glasses of wine at O'Malley's Bar. Thereafter, he asked her to exit the vehicle. She did so without using anything for support and walked in an ordinary fashion to the rear of her vehicle in front of the marked State Police car. It was at that location that Kathy was required to undergo certain field exercises to determine the level of her sobriety.

Now you will hear Trooper Long testify as to the various tests he had my client perform, and you will hear how she performed on these tests. Notably, none of these tasks consisted of natural, ordinary, everyday tasks, but rather they consisted of tasks that require a person to have agility and required physical tasks that Kathy, myself, you, and even the prosecutor probably never do in any aspect of our daily routine. These tasks included: walking heel-to-toe in a straight line, nine steps, turning around, taking heel-to-toe steps back; standing on one leg for thirty seconds with her leg about six inches off the ground and hands to the side, and then closing her eyes and tilting her head back as far as she could and trying to then touch the tip of her nose with the tip of her fingers upon the officer's command for doing same.

Despite what Trooper Long might say, we believe the evidence will show that Kathy performed those tasks remarkably well given the fact that she has never done tasks such as that, and given the fact that this was done on the side of a major highway at night with cars traveling by at significant speeds.

After my client performed those tests, the officer formed an opinion that my client was under the influence of alcohol. He arrested her and brought her back to the State Police barracks to determine her blood-alcohol content.

Now you will hear the prosecutor and the trooper talk about what Kathy's blood-alcohol content was, and they will talk about her blood-alcohol content even though they never even attempted to have Kathy's blood drawn that evening even though they were only five minutes away from a local community hospital. Rather, you will hear testimony from the trooper that my client was required to submit to a chemical test of her breath to indirectly measure the amount of alcohol that was in her blood. This, ladies and gentlemen, is an indirect test, and although it is a permissible test, we believe that upon your hearing all of the evidence, you will be left with questions regarding the reliability of that test, the accuracy of that test, and those questions will be an actual reasonable doubt that you will be left with at the end of this case.

You will also learn that this breath test has a built-in margin of error of plus or minus 0.01 of 1 percent, which is a 10 percent margin of error on either end of where Kathy's purported blood-alcohol content was as measured by her breath that evening. In other words, it could be a whole 0.02 of 1 percent variance, which means an actual 20 percent variance. You will also learn from the trooper himself that there are certain assumptions this breath test device must rely on and that there is no way for him to know if those assumptions were applicable to my client, but rather those assumptions have been applied universally to everyone even though they may not apply to all.

So what are we left with? At the end of this case, I suspect, ladies and gentlemen, that you will be left with assumptions, margins of error, and subjective opinion as to what my client's condition and blood-alcohol content was that evening. But what you will not be left with are verifiable answers from objectively established facts establishing what my client's blood-alcohol content was, and you will be left with doubts that my client was actually intoxicated from those two glasses of wine over that two and a half hour period of time on the night of her arrest.

At the conclusion of this case, when it is time for you to go back into that jury room and deliberate, you will be left with many questions, and those questions are actual real doubts you will have as to whether my client operated a motor vehicle with a blood-alcohol content of 0.08 percent or more, and whether my client had operated a motor vehicle that evening while in an intoxicated condition, and as such, we will be asking you to return a verdict of not guilty on the two counts of DWI. Thank you.

8

The Prosecutions's Direct Case: Cross-Examining the Arresting Officer

Cross-Examination of the Arresting Officer

The cross-examination of an arresting officer in a DUI case is one of the most significant portions of the DUI trial. Effective strategies in attacking the prosecution's case begin with the vehicle's operation stage.

Vehicle Operation Stage

In most DUI cases, the police stop the accused for some type of Vehicle and Traffic Law violation. Sometimes the stop is for a violation that is not considered erratic operation. One of the most common tickets written is for speeding. Notably, speeding is not one of the visual cue descriptions listed in the National Highway Traffic and Safety Administration's (NHTSA's) *DWI Detection and Standardized Field Sobriety Testing Participant Manual.* U.S.DEP'T. OF TRANSP., DWI DETECTION & STANDARDIZED FIELD SOBRIETY TESTING PARTICIPANT MANUAL (2004 ed.) at V-4 – V-7. A very effective cross-examination can be done by using your client's alleged excessive speed to your advantage. A sample cross-examination can be as follows:

> *Question:* Officer, can we agree that you observed my client speeding on the date of her arrest?
>
> *Answer:* Yes.

Question: And speeding is not just exclusive to an individual who is under the influence of alcohol?

Answer: Yes.

Question: Over the years, you have written hundreds if not thousands of speeding tickets, correct?

Answer: Yes.

Question: And almost all of those people were not under the influence of alcohol?

Answer: Yes.

Question: Can we also agree that you have probably investigated numerous auto accidents, some of which unfortunately resulted in serious physical injury or even death of a person involved in the motor vehicle accident?

Answer: Yes.

Question: And many of those involved excessive speed?

Answer: Yes.

Question: Unrelated to alcohol involvement?

Answer: Yes.

Question: We can agree that when a person is driving at a rate of speed higher than what the speed limit allows, it is more difficult for the driver to control his or her vehicle?

Answer: Yes.

> *Question:* And if a person is driving in excess of the speed limit and the person is also intoxicated, a person is even more likely to be unable to control his or her vehicle?
>
> *Answer:* Yes.
>
> *Question:* On the night of my client's arrest, she was not having any difficulty controlling her vehicle within her lane even though she was driving at an excessive speed, correct?
>
> *Answer:* Yes.
>
> *Question:* In fact, my client pulled over immediately after you activated your emergency lights?
>
> *Answer:* Yes.
>
> *Question:* And she pulled over as a reasonable and prudent driver?
>
> *Answer:* Yes.

By this line of questioning, you have effectively neutralized the prosecution's suggestion that speeding is consistent with being under the influence of alcohol. In fact, you have established that it is inconsistent with being under the influence.

The NHTSA's *DWI Detection and Standardized Field Sobriety Tests Participant Manual* lists twenty-four visual cues an officer is trained to use to detect impaired drivers. They are:

1. *Weaving:* Weaving occurs when the vehicle alternately moves toward one side of the roadway and then the other, creating a zig-zag course. The pattern of lateral movement is relatively regular as one steering correction is closely followed by another.

2. *Weaving across lane lines:* Extreme cases of weaving is when the vehicle wheels cross the lane lines before correction is made.

3. *Straddling a lane line:* The vehicle is moving straight ahead with the center or lane marker between the left-hand and right-hand wheels.

4. *Swerving:* A swerve is an abrupt turn away from a generally straight course. Swerving might occur directly after a period of drifting when the driver discovers the approach of traffic in an oncoming lane or discovers that the vehicle is going off the road. Swerving might also occur as an abrupt turn is executed to return the vehicle to the traffic lane.

5. *Turning with wide radius:* During a turn, the radius defined by the distance between the turning vehicle and the center of the turn is greater than normal. The vehicle may drive wide in a curve.

6. *Drifting:* Drifting is a straight-line movement of the vehicle at a slight angle to the roadway. As the driver approaches a marker or boundary (lane marker, center line, edge of the roadway), the direction of drift might change. The vehicle drifts across the lane marker into another lane, then the driver makes a correction and the vehicle drifts back across the lane marker. Drifting might be observed within a single lane, across lanes, across the center line, onto the shoulder, and from lane to lane.

7. *Almost striking object or vehicle:* The observed vehicle almost strikes a stationary object or another moving vehicle. Examples include: passing abnormally close to a sign, wall, building, or other object; passing abnormally close to another moving vehicle; and causing another vehicle to maneuver to avoid collision.

8. *Stopping problems (too far, too short, too jerky):* Stopping too far from a curb or at an inappropriate angle. Stopping too short or beyond the limit line at an intersection. Stopping with a jerking motion or abruptly.

9. *Accelerating or decelerating rapidly:* This cue encompasses any acceleration or deceleration that is significantly more rapid than that required by the traffic conditions. Rapid acceleration might be accompanied by breaking traction; rapid deceleration might be accompanied by an abrupt stop. Also a vehicle might alternately accelerate and decelerate rapidly.

10. *Varying speed:* Alternating between speeding up and slowing down.

11. *Slow speed (ten or more miles per hour under limit):* The observed vehicle is being driven at a speed that is more than ten miles per hour below the speed limit.

12. *Driving in opposing lanes or wrong way on one-way street:* The vehicle is observed heading into opposing or crossing traffic under one or more of the following circumstances: driving in the opposing lane; backing into traffic; failing to yield the right-of-way; driving the wrong way on a one-way street.

13. *Slow response to traffic signals:* The observed vehicle exhibits a longer-than-normal response to a change in traffic signal. For example, the driver remains stopped at the intersection for an abnormally long period of time after the traffic signal has turned green.

14. *Slow or failure to respond to officer's signals:* Driver is unusually slow to respond to an officer's lights, siren, or hand signals.

15. *Stopping in lane for no apparent reason:* The critical element in this cue is that there is no observable justification for the vehicle to stop in the traffic lane; the stop is not caused by traffic conditions, traffic signals, an emergency situation, or related circumstances. Impaired drivers might stop in the lane when their capability to interpret information and make decisions becomes impaired. As a consequence, stopping in lane for no apparent reason is likely to occur at intersections or other decision points.

16. *Driving without headlights at night:* The observed vehicle is being driven with both headlights off during a period of the day when the use of headlights is required.

17. *Failure to signal or signal inconsistent with action:* A number of possibilities exist for the driver's signaling to be inconsistent with the associated driving actions. This cue occurs when inconsistencies such as the following are observed: failing to signal a turn or lane change; signaling opposite to the turn or lane change executed; signaling constantly with no accompanying driving action; and driving with four-way hazard flashers on.

18. *Following too closely:* The vehicle is observed following another vehicle while not maintaining the legal minimum separation.

19. *Improper or unsafe lane change:* Driver taking risks or endangering others. Driver is frequently or abruptly changing lanes without regard to other motorists.

20. *Illegal or improper turn (too fast, jerky, sharp, etc.):* The driver executes any turn that is abnormally abrupt or illegal. Specific examples include: turning with excessive speed, turning sharply from the wrong lane, making a U-turn illegally, and turning from outside a designated turn lane.

21. *Driving on other than designated roadway:* The vehicle is observed being driven on other than the roadway designated for traffic movement. Examples include driving at the edge of the roadway, on the shoulder, off the roadway entirely, and straight through turn-only lanes or areas.

22. *Stopping inappropriately in response to officer:* The observed vehicle stops at an inappropriate location or under inappropriate conditions, other than in the traffic lane. Examples include stopping in a prohibited zone, at a crosswalk, far short of an intersection, on a walkway, across lanes, for a green traffic signal, for a flashing yellow traffic signal, abruptly as if startled, or in an illegal, dangerous manner.

23. *Inappropriate or unusual behavior (throwing objects, arguing, etc.):* This includes throwing objects from the vehicle, drinking in the vehicle,

urinating at roadside, arguing without cause, and other disorderly actions.

24. *Appearing to be impaired:* This cue is actually one or more of a set of indicators related to the personal behavior or appearance of the driver. Examples of specific indicators might include:

- Eye fixation
- Tightly gripping the steering wheel
- Slouching in the seat
- Gesturing erratically or obscenely
- Face close to the windshield
- Driver's head protruding from vehicle

See PARTICIPANT MANUAL (2004 ed.) at V-4 – V-7.

If your client is charged with a Vehicle and Traffic Law violation that is considered to be erratic operation, it is important to neutralize the effect of the erratic operation. This can be accomplished several ways along the following line of questioning.

> *Question:* During the period of time you observed my client operating a motor vehicle, the only violation you observed was my client driving over the white line for two seconds for the entire ninety seconds you were following him?
>
> *Answer:* Yes.
>
> *Question:* Were you able to see my client's face while following him?
>
> *Answer:* No.
>
> *Question:* We can agree that you didn't know where he was looking?
>
> *Answer:* Correct.

Question: You can't tell us if he was looking at the radio to change the station?

Answer: No.

Question: Were you in a marked police vehicle?

Answer: Yes.

Question: Can you tell us if he was looking in his rearview mirror at your marked police car that was following him?

Answer: No.

Question: In your experience as a driver, taking your eyes off the road can cause a driver to fail to stay completely within the lane?

Answer: Yes.

Question: And that can be unrelated to being under the influence of alcohol?

Answer: Yes.

The above are just a few examples of how you can neutralize or at least lessen the significance of your client's underlying traffic ticket(s) as it relates to the offense of DUI.

The Stop

With regard to the actual stop, it is important for you to question the officer about there not being anything unusual about the stop both in terms of how long it took your client to stop the motor vehicle in response to the overhead traffic lights being activated, and the manner in which he or she pulled over in terms of his or her ability to control the motor vehicle. It is critically important that you question the officer about those facts at the pre-trial suppression hearing in order to know what his or her answer will be at trial. That is, if the officer indicated that your client did not stop right away and the officer had to follow him or her for a significant period of time and put on the sirens to get him or her to stop, that is something you will want to minimize at trial. In addition, if the officer testifies that your client was having difficulty controlling his or her vehicle during the stop, such as striking the curb or driving onto the sidewalk, that is also something you will want to know about ahead of time to minimize that damage at trial.

Driver Contact Stage

In DUI prosecutions, the prosecutor will question the arresting officer with regard to the observations the officer made during the period of time the officer was interacting with your client. Typically, these observations include the manner of your client's speech; whether the officer detected an odor of an alcoholic beverage emanating from your client's breath; observations regarding whether your client's eyes were bloodshot and glassy; and whether the officer observed any impaired motor coordination when the driver provided license and registration documentation.

Left unchallenged, the prosecution will be able to greatly improve the chance of securing a DUI common law conviction by proffering such evidence. It thus becomes vital to challenge the officer's observations.

Odor of Alcoholic Beverage

Challenging the officer's testimony that he or she detected an odor of an alcoholic beverage on your client's breath begins with an understanding that the type of alcohol in alcoholic beverages is ethyl alcohol. Moreover, ethanol is an odorless type of substance. Getting the officer to concede this effectively allows you to proceed with a line of questioning that will neutralize the significance of the presence of an odor of an alcoholic beverage. A line of questioning as follows helps demonstrate the point:

> *Question:* Officer, can we agree that the type of alcohol in intoxicating beverages is ethyl alcohol?
>
> *Answer:* Yes.

Question: And in fact, ethyl alcohol is an odorless type of substance?

Answer: Yes.

Question: If ethanol is odorless, then a trained officer such as yourself cannot determine from the odor alone what a person had to drink, correct?

Answer: Yes.

Question: Or how much alcohol the person drank?

Answer: Correct.

Question: Or when the person first consumed the alcoholic beverage?

Answer: Correct.

Question: Or when the person last consumed the alcoholic beverage?

Answer: Yes.

Question: Can we agree, officer, that depending on how recently it was consumed, as little as one alcoholic beverage (whether it be a glass of wine or one beer) can still leave a strong odor of an alcoholic beverage on a subject's breath?

Answer: Yes.

Question: Such that if a person had one beer one hour before coming into your presence, that person would have a strong odor of an alcoholic beverage emanating from his or her breath?

Answer: Yes.

Question: So we can agree that standing alone, a strong odor of an alcoholic beverage tells us nothing about how much alcohol a person consumed.

Answer: Yes.

(If the officer denies this, proceed along the following lines.)

Question: Officer, if I were to take a swig of beer and swish it around in my mouth and spit it out, I would have an odor of an alcoholic beverage on my breath, correct?

Answer: Yes.

Question: And depending on how recently I had swished it in my mouth, it may very well leave a strong odor of an alcoholic beverage on my breath?

Answer: Yes.

Question: And we can agree that would be true even though I had never actually consumed or swallowed any alcohol, correct?

Answer: Yes.

Question: Therefore, you would agree that the odor of an alcoholic beverage tells us nothing about how much a person had to drink?

Answer: Yes.

Slurred Speech

Slurred speech is a classic sign of being under the influence of alcohol. Almost anyone who has seen an intoxicated individual will equate slurred speech as a symptom of being under the influence of alcohol.

The reality of most DUI prosecutions is that the arresting officer will testify that your client's speech was slurred. To help minimize the impact of this evidence, we will directly confront the officer as to whether he or she had ever met your client prior to the night of the arrest. Almost always the answer is no. Once you have established this, the officer will have to concede that he or she is not certain of how your client normally speaks. The following is an example of cross-examination on this issue:

> *Question:* Officer, since you never met my client prior to her arrest, you don't know the normal manner of her speech, correct?
>
> *Answer:* Yes.
>
> *Question:* You don't know whether she speaks with any type of impediment?
>
> *Answer:* No.
>
> *Question:* Were you able to understand everything she was articulating to you on the night of her arrest?
>
> *Answer:* Yes.
>
> *Question:* We can agree then that there was nothing my client stated that you were not able to understand?
>
> *Answer:* Correct.
>
> *Question:* We can also agree that all of her answers were logically responsive to the questions asked of her?
>
> *Answer:* Yes.
>
> *Question:* You characterized her speech as being slurred?
>
> *Answer:* Yes.

Question: What was the first word you heard her slur?

Answer: I don't recall.

Question: What was the last word you heard her slur?

Answer: I don't recall.

Question: What was any word you heard her slur?

Answer: I don't recall.

Question: So then, although you cannot recall a single word my client slurred, you are still telling this jury/judge that my client spoke with slurred speech?

Answer: Yes.

Note that you should always first explore this line of questioning at a pre-trial suppression hearing. In the event that hearing testimony reveals that the officer recalls what word(s) your client slurred, you should not explore this specific line of questioning at trial. In our experience, the arresting officer will seldom recall what words the client slurred.

Bloodshot Eyes

Bloodshot eyes is also a common characteristic of an individual who is under the influence of alcohol. There are, however, several other causes of bloodshot eyes that are completely unrelated to being under the influence of alcohol.

During the cross-examination of the arresting officer relative to bloodshot eyes, it is important to establish that the officer is unilaterally concluding that your client's eyes were bloodshot because your client is under the influence of alcohol. Put another way, the officer is not considering other causes of the bloodshot eyes. By highlighting to the jury that the officer is assuming the eyes are bloodshot because of alcohol consumption without exploring other possible causes, it can lead to the conclusion that the officer is not giving your client a fair shake. Examples of how to effectively question the arresting officer follow:

> *Question:* Officer, we can agree that you observed my client with bloodshot eyes on the evening of her arrest?
>
> *Answer:* Yes.
>
> *Question:* And you relied on that in forming your opinion that my client was intoxicated?
>
> *Answer:* Yes.
>
> *Question:* You learned in your training as well as through your common experiences that there can be other causes of bloodshot eyes unrelated to alcohol consumption, correct?.
>
> *Answer:* Yes.
>
> *Question:* One of those causes could be allergies?
>
> *Answer:* Yes.
>
> *Question:* Another can be smoke sensitivity?
>
> *Answer:* Yes.
>
> *Question:* Another could be lack of sleep?
>
> *Answer:* Yes.
>
> *Question:* You learned in your training that in a DWI investigation or any criminal investigation, it is critically important to be as thorough as possible, correct?
>
> *Answer:* Yes.

Question: And you strive to accomplish that objective in all of your cases?

Answer: Yes.

Question: And you did so in this investigation as well, correct?

Answer: Yes.

Question: Did you inquire of my client if she suffered from any allergies on the night of her arrest?

Answer: No.

Question: Did you inquire of my client if she had been exposed to any smoke on the night of her arrest?

Answer: No.

Question: Please tell the jury/court how many hours it had been since my client had last slept prior to the night of her arrest.

Answer: I don't know.

Question: We can agree that the reason you don't know is because you never asked her that question?

Answer: Yes.

Question: And we can further agree that it is an important question to ask in a DWI investigation.

Answer: Yes.

By following this line of questioning, you are able to eliminate or at least neutralize the impact of the officer's observations of your client and thereby help create a reasonable doubt with regard to the officer's opinion that your client was intoxicated.

Field Sobriety Testing: Cross-Examination by the Book

One of the most defensible aspects of any DUI case is the field sobriety test evidence. Mounting a proper defense to any DWI case requires the practitioner to be familiarized with the National Highway Traffic Safety Administration's (NHTSA) standardized field sobriety tests. These are set forth in the 2002, 2004, and 2006 editions of the NHTSA's *Field Sobriety Testing Manual.*

Police use field sobriety tests to help them form an opinion as to whether they have reasonable cause to believe a subject is under the influence of alcohol. If an officer has reasonable cause to believe a subject is intoxicated or impaired, he or she has the right to ask the person to submit to a chemical test of his or her blood, breath, urine, or saliva pursuant to NY VEH & TRAF § 1194.

When you begin to question the arresting officer about the field sobriety tests, get the officer to concede that he or she is giving your client field sobriety tests to help assess your client's natural motor coordination skills to assist in determining whether your client can operate a motor vehicle as a reasonable and prudent driver. In reality, the field sobriety tests consist of mostly unnatural acts. That is, the officer is attempting to assess your client's natural motor coordination skills by having your client perform unnatural acts. Highlighting that to the trier of fact helps you lessen the impact of negative field sobriety test evidence.

There are three standardized field sobriety tests as established by the NHTSA: the horizontal gaze nystagmus (HGN) test, the walk-and-turn test, and the one-leg stand test.

The Horizontal Gaze Nystagmus Test

Nystagmus is defined as an involuntary jerking of the eyes. Nystagmus can be caused by certain physical disorders, including brain tumors and other brain damage or some diseases of the inner ear. *See* PARTICIPANT MANUAL (2004 ed.) at VIII-4.

To administer the HGN test, the eyes are checked for equal pupil size, resting nystagmus, and equal tracking, as to whether they can follow an object. As noted in the manual, if the eyes do not track together or if the pupils are noticeably unequal in size, there is a chance that medical disorders or injuries causing nystagmus are present. *Id.* at VIII-5.

A police officer will attempt to use the HGN test in forming an opinion as to your client's condition. The HGN test looks for an involuntary jerking of the eyes occurring as the eyes gaze towards the side. This test looks for three clues. The first clue is lack of smooth pursuit. This clue attempts to determine whether the eyes can be observed to balance as they follow a smoothly moving stimulus such as a pencil or penlight. The manual notes that the eyes of an unimpaired person will follow smoothly, such as a marble rolling across a smooth pane of glass or windshield wipers moving across a wet windshield. *Id.* at VIII-5.

The second clue is distinct and sustained nystagmus at maximum deviation. This clue looks to see whether there is distinct and sustained nystagmus when the eye is held at maximum deviation for a minimum of four seconds. *Id.* at VIII-5.

The third clue is the onset of nystagmus prior to forty-five degrees. This clue looks for whether there is nystagmus (jerking) prior to forty-five degrees. *See 2004 Participant Manual* VIII-5. How far the stimulus is placed from the subject's nose is a critical factor in estimating the forty-five-degree angle. That is, if the stimulus is held twelve inches in front of the suspect's nose, it should be moved twelve inches to the side to reach forty-five degrees. Likewise, if the stimulus is held fifteen inches in front of the suspect's nose, it should be moved fifteen inches to the side to reach forty-five degrees. *Id.* at VIII-6.

The administration of any field sobriety test must be done precisely according to the instruction manual. Notably, the NHTSA mandates that the tests are to be administered in the prescribed standardized manner, and if any one of these standardized field sobriety test elements is changed, the validity of the test is compromised. *Id.* at VIII-19.

To administer the HGN test, the officer will tell the subject, "I'm going to check your eyes," "Keep your head still and follow the stimulus with your eyes only," and "Keep following the stimulus with your eyes until I tell you to stop." *See 2004 Participant Manual* VIII-6. The manual then requires the officer to position the stimulus approximately twelve to fifteen inches from the subject's nose and slightly above eye level. The officer then must check to see that both pupils are equal in size. The officer then must check the suspect's eyes for the ability to track together. This is done by moving the stimulus smoothly across the suspect's entire field of vision. The officer must check to see if the eyes track the stimulus together or if one lags behind the other. If the eyes do not track together, it could indicate the possibility of a medical disorder, injury, or blindness. *Id.* at VIII-6.

Thereafter, the officer must check the suspect's left eye by moving the stimulus to his or her right. The stimulus must be moved smoothly at a speed that requires approximately two seconds to bring the suspect's eye as far to the side as it can go. While moving the stimulus, the officer must look at the suspect's eye to determine whether he or she is able to pursue smoothly. The officer then must move the stimulus all the way to the left back across the suspect's face, checking to see if the right eye pursues smoothly. Movement of the stimulus should take approximately two seconds out and two second back for each eye, and then the procedure is repeated. *Id.* at VIII-7.

Thereafter, the officer must check the eyes for distinct and sustained nystagmus at maximum deviation. Beginning with the left eye, the officer moves the object to the suspect's left side until the eye has gone as far to the side as possible. Usually there will be no white showing in the corner of the eye at maximum deviation. The officer must hold the eye at that position for a minimum of four seconds and observe the eye for distinct and sustained nystagmus. The officer then must move the stimulus all the way across the suspect's face to check the right eye, holding it at a position for a minimum of four seconds. That procedure is repeated. *Id.* at VIII-7.

Thereafter, the officer must check for the third clue, which is the onset of nystagmus prior to forty-five degrees. This is done by starting to move the stimulus towards the right, which is the suspect's left eye, at a speed that would take approximately four seconds for the stimulus to reach the edge of a suspect's shoulder. The officer must watch the eye carefully for any sign of jerking. When the officer sees any sign of jerking, he or she must stop and verify that the jerking continues. The officer then moves the stimulus to the left (a suspect's right eye) at a speed that would take approximately four seconds for the stimulus to reach the edge of a suspect's shoulder. Again, the officer must watch the eye carefully for any sign of jerking. When the officer observes it, he or she must stop and verify that the jerking continues. The officer must repeat the procedure. *Id.* at VIII-7.

Test Interpretation

The officer is trained to look for three clues of nystagmus in each eye: whether the eye cannot follow the moving object smoothly, whether nystagmus is distinct and sustained when the eye is held at maximum deviation for a minimum of four seconds, and whether the angle of onset of nystagmus is prior to forty-five degrees. According to research, if four or more clues are present, it is likely that the suspect's blood-alcohol content is above 0.10. According to the NHTSA, using this criterion, officers will be able to classify about 77 percent of their suspects accurately. *Id.* at VIII-8.

The Walk-and-Turn Test

The walk-and-turn test is a standardized field sobriety test that has a suspect assume a heel-to-toe stance while being given verbal instructions. The subject is to place his or her left foot on a line (either a real or imaginary line) and then place the right foot on the line ahead of the left foot, with the heel of the right foot against the toe of the left foot. The subject is then told to place his or her arms down at his or her side and to maintain that position until the officer has completed the instructions. The officer will repeat, "Do not start to walk until told to do so." The officer then will ask the subject if he or she understands the instructions.

The officer then will instruct and demonstrate the walk-and-turn test. The instructions are as follows: The officer will tell the subject that upon his or her telling the subject to start, the subject is to take nine heel-to-toe steps, turn, and take nine heel-to-toe steps back. (The officer will demonstrate three heel-to-toe steps.) The officer will instruct the subject on the turn by advising the subject to keep the front foot on the line and to turn by taking a series of small steps with the other foot while demonstrating. The officer will instruct the subject that while walking, he or she is to keep his or her hands at the sides and watch his or her feet at all times, and count steps out loud. The officer will also instruct the subject that once he or she starts walking, he or she should not stop until they have completed the test. The officer is then instructed to ask the subject if he or she understood the instructions. Upon the subject acknowledging that he or she understands the instructions, the subject is told to begin and to count the first step from the heel-to-toe position as one. *Id.* at VIII-9.

Test Interpretation

The officers are looking for the following eight clues:

1. The suspect cannot keep balance during the instructional stage. Notably, this clue is only to be recorded if the suspect does not maintain heel-to-toe position throughout the instructions. That is, the feet must actually break apart. The officer is not allowed to record this as a clue if the suspect sways or uses the arms for balance but maintains a heel-to-toe position during the instructional stage.
2. The suspect starts before the instructions are finished.
3. The suspect stops while walking. For this clue to be valid, the suspect must pause for several seconds. An officer is not allowed to record this clue if the suspect is merely walking slowly.
4. The suspect does not touch heel-to-toe. This clue is only valid if the suspect leaves a space of more than one-half inch between the heel and the toe on any given step.
5. The suspect steps off line. This is only a clue if the suspect steps so that one foot is completely off the line.
6. The suspect uses his or her arms for balance. For this clue to be valid, the suspect must raise one or both arms more than six inches from the sides to maintain balance.
7. Improper turn. The suspect removes the front foot from the line while turning. In addition, this may also be recorded as a clue if the suspect does not follow the directions as to how the turn was demonstrated, and the suspect spins or pivots around. During the instructional stage, the suspect is taught that instead of pivoting, he or she is to take short, choppy steps and turn.

8. The eighth and final clue is whether the suspect takes the incorrect number of steps. That is, the suspect takes more or fewer than nine steps in either direction.

Id. at VIII-10, VIII-11.

According to the NHTSA manual, if a suspect exhibits two or more clues on this test or fails to complete it, the officer may classify the suspect's blood-alcohol content as above 0.10. Using these clues, the manual alleges that the officer will be able to accurately classify 68 percent of their suspects. *Id.* at VIII-11.

Test Conditions for the Walk-and-Turn Test

The walk-and-turn test requires a designated straight line and should be conducted on a reasonably dry, hard, level, non-slippery surface. There should be sufficient room for the suspect to complete nine heel-to-toe steps. With regard to the test conditions, research has indicated that individuals over sixty-five years of age or who have back, leg, or middle ear problems have difficulty performing the test. In addition, individuals who are wearing heels of more than two inches should be given the opportunity to remove their shoes to complete the test. *Id.* at VIII-11.

If a police officer combines four or more clues of the HGN test with two or more clues of the walk-and-turn test, he or she can classify the suspect as having above a 0.10 blood-alcohol content 86 percent of the time. *Id.*

When cross-examining police officers with regard to the walk-and-turn test, it is essential to confront them with the fact that although a particular clue may appear several times, it still only constitutes one clue. *Id.* at VIII-19. In addition, it is also important to get the officer to concede that the test results for all standardized field sobriety tests are only valid when the tests "are administered in the prescribed, standardized manner; the standardized clues are used to assess the suspect's performance; and the standardized criteria are employed to interpret that performance." The manual states, "If any one of the standardized field sobriety tests elements is changed, the validity is compromised." *Id.*

As such, when cross-examining the arresting officer on the walk-and-turn test, it is essential for counsel to take the officer through questioning whereby he or she describes in great detail every specific instruction he or she gave to your client. It is essential to have the *DWI Detection and Standardized Field Sobriety Testing Participant Manual* to effectively cross-examine the officer. Notably, with all standardized field sobriety tests or even non-standardized field sobriety tests, individuals are only being scored in the negative. That is, they only lose points for things they do incorrectly. They do not, however, receive points for any portion of the test they do correctly. It is helpful to break down the number of tasks our clients do correctly on any given field sobriety test. Then, when the officer testifies to what the person did negatively, the positive aspects of the tests significantly outweigh the negative aspects of the tests, and from a percentage perspective, you can establish to the trier of fact that your client has actually done 70 percent and sometimes more of the tests correctly. When it comes time to give your summation to the jury, you can use analogies. For example, if your child came home from school and was told that he or she did 80 or 85 percent of the test correctly and received a failing grade, would that seem unfair to you? Using this type of example as well as others can effectively drive home the point to the jury that these tests are inherently unfair and should not be credited in determining whether your client was intoxicated or impaired by alcohol.

The One-Leg Stand Test

The third standardized field sobriety test is the one-leg stand test. The one-leg stand test is initiated by the officer giving the suspect the following instructions: (1) The suspect is to stand with his or her feet together and arms down at his or her side. (2) The suspect is told to not start to perform the test until he or she is told to do so. (3) The suspect is asked if he or she understands the instructions so far. The officer then will demonstrate and give instructions for the one-leg stand test. The officer will tell the suspect that upon his or her command, the suspect is to raise one leg, whichever one he or she feels most comfortable raising, with the foot approximately six inches off the ground and keeping the foot raised parallel to the ground. The suspect is also advised that he or she must keep both legs straight and arms to his or her side. The officer will then tell the suspect that while holding that position, he or she is to count out loud in the following manner: one thousand and one, one thousand and two, one thousand and three, etc. until told when to stop.

The suspect is also told that he or she is to keep arms at his or her sides at all times and to keep watching the raised foot. The suspect is then asked if he or she understands the instructions, and then the suspect is told to begin the test. If the suspect puts the foot down at any point during the test, the suspect is told to pick the foot up again and continue counting from the point at which the foot touched the ground. The officer is instructed that if the suspect counts slowly, terminate the test after thirty seconds. *Id.* at VIII-12.

Test Interpretation

According to NHTSA research, if two or more clues are present, there is a good chance that the blood-alcohol content is above 0.10 percent. Using the criteria listed in the manual, the officer will be able to classify 65 percent of the people they have tested as to whether their blood-alcohol contents are above 0.10. *Id.* at VIII-13. The clues the officer is trained to look for are:

1. Suspect sways while balancing. This refers to a side-to-side or back-and-forth motion while the suspect maintains the one-leg stand position.
2. The suspect uses arms for balance. This clue is indicated if the suspect moves his or her arms six inches or more from the side of the body to keep balance.
3. Hopping. This clue is indicated if the suspect is able to keep one foot off the ground but resorts to hopping to maintain balance.
4. Puts foot down. This clue is indicated if the suspect is unable to maintain the one-leg stand position, putting the foot down one or more times during the thirty-second count.

See PARTICIPANT MANUAL (2004 ed.). According to the NHTSA manual, original research has shown that persons with blood-alcohol contents of 0.10 can maintain balance for up to twenty-five seconds but seldom as long as thirty.

Test Conditions

The one-leg stand requires a reasonably dry, hard, level, and non-slippery surface, and research indicates that certain individuals over sixty-five years of age or with back, leg, or middle ear problems, or people who are overweight by fifty or more pounds, have difficulty performing the test. In addition, individuals wearing heels more than two inches high should be given the opportunity to remove their shoes while taking the test. *Id.* at VIII-13 – VIII-14.

When cross-examining an officer relative to the one-leg stand test, it is imperative to educate the jury or judge that standing with one leg raised in the air and having to balance in that position is an unnatural act. The following can be a sample cross-examination of the one-leg stand test:

> *Question:* Officer, can we agree that it is not natural for a person to stand with one leg in the air?
>
> *Answer:* Yes.
>
> *Question:* Officer, in fact, other than in the course of your duties as a police officer when you are demonstrating the one-leg stand to individuals who are under investigation for DWI, you don't stand on one leg for any other purpose, correct?
>
> *Answer:* Correct.
>
> *Question:* And can we agree that during the field sobriety testing, you are attempting to assess my client's natural motor coordination skills to determine whether he is capable of operating a vehicle as a reasonable and prudent driver?
>
> *Answer:* Yes.
>
> *Question:* Then you would agree with me that although you are attempting to assess my client's natural motor coordination skills, you are asking him to do unnatural acts of balancing on one leg?
>
> *Answer:* Yes.

Question: And we can agree that you have had a valid license for a number of years?

Answer: Yes.

Question: And prior to obtaining your license, you had to take a road test through the Department of Motor Vehicles?

Answer: Yes.

Question: And can we agree that during that road test you were never required to stand on one leg to obtain your driver's license?

Answer: Yes.

Question: Can we also agree, officer, that at no point in time during any testing procedure in the course of you getting your driver's license were you ever required to balance on one leg?

Answer: Correct.

Question: And you're not aware of any type of Department of Motor Vehicles regulation or requirement that a suspect has to be able to stand on one leg and keep his balance for thirty seconds before he is determined to be capable of driving?

Answer: No.

By using this type of questioning, you can effectively reduce the significance of a poor performance on the one-leg stand test. In addition, as noted with regard to the walk-and-turn test, it is important to emphasize to the trier of fact that a suspect is only being deducted points on the one-leg stand test and is not receiving any positive points for things he or she did correctly during the test.

Also, when questioning the arresting officer for all field sobriety tests, it is important to bring out through cross-examination that it is not unusual for individuals to be nervous during police and citizen encounters, even when they are stopped for a simple speeding ticket. Thus, you can argue to the jury that people perform differently under stressful conditions and normally stress causes people to react in a negative fashion more than a positive fashion.

Non-standardized Field Sobriety Tests

Non-standardized field sobriety tests are tests that have not been standardized by the NHTSA. These tests are typically the alphabet test, the countdown test, the finger count test, the finger-to-nose test, and the rhomberg test. The 2004 edition of the *DWI Detection and Standardized Field Sobriety Testing Participant Manual* discusses the alphabet, countdown, and finger count tests. *See* PARTICIPANT MANUAL (2004 ed.) at VI-5, VI-6. Significantly, the manual indicates that these type of techniques are not as reliable as standardized field sobriety tests, but they can still be useful for the detection of impairment. The manual notes that these tests do not replace the standardized field sobriety tests. *Id.* at VI-4. By confronting the arresting officer with that language, you will have the officer in a position that recognizes that those tests are not as reliable as the standardized field sobriety tests. With that in mind, if you are able to impeach the reliability of the HGN, walk-and-turn, and one-leg stand standardized field sobriety tests, you will be able to argue that if the standardized field sobriety tests are not reliable, the non-standardized field sobriety tests cannot be reliable, as the officer's training manual teaches him or her that those tests are not as reliable as the standardized field sobriety tests.

We have included a sample cross-examination of an arresting officer as Appendix D. This examination is factually specific to the facts involved in that case and is provided merely for guidance purposes. Each DUI case is unique based upon its own facts and circumstances, and your cross-examination should be tailored to those facts.

9

Cross-Examination of the Breath Test Operator

There are two breath testing devices used in our jurisdiction. They are the Data Master and the Draeger AlcoTest 9510. These two breath test devices use infrared spectroscopy. In very simple terms, this works by having infrared energy measure compounds present in the human breath. Infrared energy will be absorbed by a molecule of a given compound at different levels (wavelengths). The level at which the infrared energy is being absorbed identifies the compound. Typically, alcohol will absorb radiation at wavelengths of approximately 3.0, 3.9, 7.25, 9.18, 9.5, and 11.5 microns. A micron is a linear measurement of electromagnetic radiation.

Infrared energy will be absorbed by the alcohol vapor it passes. This is accomplished by the infrared device passing infrared light through the sample of the defendant's breath. Alcohol that is present in the sample will be absorbed by the infrared energy at a particular wavelength being utilized by the instrument. The Data Master utilizes a 3.4 micron range, whereas the Draeger AlcoTest uses the 9.5 micron range. The theory behind the Draeger utilizing the 9.5 range is due to the fact that acetone, which is a compound commonly found in human breath, absorbs infrared light in the 3.4 micron range. With regard to the Data Master 3.37 and 3.44, alcohol will absorb infrared light at both levels but acetone will differ at each level.

Defenses to Breath Tests

The Principle of Breath Testing Is That It Is an Indirect Measurement of Blood Alcohol by Measuring Breath Alcohol

A breath test is not and will never be a direct measurement of one's blood-alcohol level. Breath testing is based upon Henry's Law. Henry's Law states that there is a relationship between a volatile chemical substance in liquid state and the same volatile chemical substance in vapor state, and whatever that relationship is, it is directly affected by changes in temperature.

Blood/Breath Conversion Factor

All breath testing devices assume that the concentration of alcohol in a person's blood equals the concentration of alcohol present in 2,100 milliliters of air. The same weight of alcohol will be contained in one cubic centimeter of pulmonary blood as in 2.1 liters of deep lung breath. *See* LAWRENCE E. TAYLOR & STEVEN OBERMAN, DRUNK DRIVING DEFENSE 395 (6th ed. 2006). Ultimately, the number obtained or being read as ethanol through the breath testing device is multiplied by 2,100 (the conversion factor) and then reported as grams per 210 liters of breath.

The fact of the matter is that nobody knows for certain what any given person's blood/breath conversion factor is. It can range anywhere between 1 to 1,100 and 1 to 3,000. *See Id.* The lower the partition ratio, the higher the breath test reading on a properly functioning breath test machine. The higher the partition ratio, a lower breath test reading will result on a properly functioning breath test machine.

Body Temperature Defense

The body temperature defense relates to the 1 to 2,100 relationship. The 1 to 2,100 relationship depends on the temperature of breath being 34 degrees centigrade. If the breath temperature of a subject is greater than 34 degrees centigrade, a higher blood-alcohol content will be reported on the breath test device.

Using the Simulator Solution to Establish the Body Temperature Defense

A simulator solution must be 34 degrees centigrade plus or minus 0.2 of a degree. The simulator solution simulates a person taking the test. The breath test operator must discard the simulator solution if it is outside 34 degrees centigrade plus or minus 0.2 of a degree. During cross-examination of the breath test operator, you can easily get him or her to concede that as little as an increase of 0.3 of a degree will result in an erroneously high test result that will invalidate the test result. You can then attack the entire test as being unreliable by asking the police officer if he or she took the defendant's temperature. An experienced or well-trained police officer who is knowledgeable of breath test issues may know there is only approximately a 6.5 percent error per degree centigrade increase or decrease in the known body temperature. *See Id.* at 440–441.

The Simulator Defense

All breath testing devices have a built-in simulator defense as well. Depending on what the reference standard is, the simulator solution must contain a reportable value of plus or minus 0.01 of that known reference standard. A simulator solution is used to test the accuracy of the instrument. The State Police do not run weekly simulator tests. However, the local police departments using the Data Master do. The weekly simulator tests can be very effective in building a line of questioning as to the number of tests that are run by police agencies at a given time in order to establish the accuracy of the breath test device. That is, typically the weekly simulator tests are run by town and village police departments on the Data Master. There are typically three tests conducted. In contrast, when a subject is arrested and takes a chemical test, only one breath sample is secured and analyzed. The same is true with the Draeger. New York State Department of Health Rules and Regulations do not require more than one sample being taken. As such, although the Data Master is using infrared energy at two different wavelengths, and even though the Draeger AlcoTest is utilizing infrared energy at 9.5 micron wavelength as well as the fuel cell technology, you must remember and it must be brought out to the jury that only one sample of the defendant's breath is being secured and analyzed. This can be particularly effective in that on both the AlcoTest and the Data Master, two blank tests are run as well as two simulator tests during the breath testing of the subject. In fact, it would take very little time and no expense to run a second test on the subject.

Moreover, as far as a simulator defense, the simulator solution must have a certain degree of tolerance. That is, it must be within plus or minus 0.01 of the known reference standard at 34 degrees plus or minus 0.02 of 1 degree. As such, there is a range of error of 20 percent. This range exists without even taking into consideration any other potential malfunction of the device or any other type of inherent problem in the device. Once you establish that point, you can use different analogies for the jury based on that range of error. For example, does the government allow you to pay 90 percent of your tax liability, or do they require you to pay 100 percent?

Mouth Alcohol Defense

The twenty-minute waiting period that is required by most departments (the New York State Department of Health Rules and Regulations require a minimum of fifteen minutes) is designed to eliminate any type of residual mouth alcohol present that could contaminate the air sample being analyzed by the breath test machine. The infrared breath test devices have built-in slope detectors. The purpose of a slope detector is to determine whether the breath sample being captured has been contaminated by mouth alcohol. The way slope detectors work is that the device measures the concentration of alcohol that is in the breath sample. The theory behind the slope detector is that the deep lung air has the highest concentration of alcohol, whereby the alcohol coming from the throat and mouth should contain less of a concentration of alcohol. As such, there should be a gradual increase in slope of the blood-alcohol content as the person blows. The theory of the slope detector is that if there is any type of residual mouth alcohol that is being measured, the sample will start off with too high of a BAC that will then slope downwards as the person continues to blow. When the breath test device detects a slope in that regard, it declares a sample to be invalid and will abort the test.

What Was the Blood-Alcohol Content at the Time of Operation?

This is the ultimate issue in any DUI breath or blood test case. New York State is still a blood alcohol state and not a breath alcohol state. As such, the prosecution needs to establish what the client's blood-alcohol content was at the time of operation and not at time of breath test.

Typically, the breath test operator will concede that he or she is not an expert as to how the machine works, only that he or she is qualified to operate the machine. Along the same lines, when cross-examining the breath test operator, get him or her to concede that he or she is not an expert on human physiology, toxicology, or pharmacology, and that he or she cannot calculate or estimate what a person's blood-alcohol content was other than what the machine purports it to be. Interestingly, the breath test operator will almost always concede that he or she cannot state what a person's blood-alcohol content was at time of operation. Depending on what your client's breath test result was and when the sample was taken in relation to the time of operation, you have credible facts to argue to the jury that there is reasonable doubt.

The Test Can't Be Right Defense

This defense simply is that the common law evidence does not match the blood-alcohol content. This is typically used in cases where there is a high blood-alcohol content and the defendant performs well on field sobriety tests and no erratic operation is observed. Your client's conduct and operation of the motor vehicle is not consistent with what most typical jurors would expect of an intoxicated driver. You establish these facts to support this defense through the cross-examination of the arresting officer. In addition, if there is a videotape of the field sobriety tests, that can also be used to support this defense.

Breath Test Observation Periods

Most police agencies require a minimum fifteen- to twenty-minute waiting period prior to the administration of any type of chemical test to ensure that the subject has been observed during that period. 10 NYCRR 59.5(b) requires that police maintain a continuous observation of the subject for fifteen minutes prior to the collection of the breath sample, during which time the subject must not have ingested alcoholic beverages or other fluids, regurgitated, vomited, eaten, smoked, or been allowed to place anything in his or her mouth. If the subject should regurgitate, vomit, smoke, or place anything in his or her mouth, an additional fifteen-minute waiting period shall be required. Recently there have been cases from the New York State Supreme Court Appellate Term for the Ninth and Tenth Judicial District that have held that noncompliance with the rules and regulations of the Department of Health go to the weight of the evidence and not the admissibility of the breath test result. *See People v. Schuessler*, 829 N.Y.S.2d 808 (2006); *see also People v. Lebrecht*, 823 N.Y.S.2d 824 (2006).

Although these cases do hold that noncompliance with the observation period does not affect admissibility, counsel should nevertheless still attempt to cross-examine the breath test operator on the failure to observe the subject so that you may still argue to the trier of fact that there is a reason why the fact finder should not accept the breath test result as reliable.

Calibration Records and Right to Confrontation

People v. Lebrecht, 823 N.Y.S.2d 824 (2006), held that certified copies of breath test calibration records do not violate the confrontation clause and the principles under *Crawford v. Washington*, 541 US 36 (2004).

Keeping the Breath Test out Through Discovery Violations

Any attorney who is representing an individual accused of DUI where there is a chemical test result must make a specific demand to produce seeking discovery of all calibration and maintenance records for the breath test device and all simulator test certifications as well as weekly simulator test results. The New York State Police do not run weekly simulator tests on the simulator solution. All county, town, village, and city police departments who use the Data Master run weekly simulator tests. In our experience, the prosecution will seldom turn over those weekly simulator tests, notwithstanding the fact that we demand them in a demand to produce.

The people's failure to supply those weekly simulator test results can serve as a viable basis to move to preclude the breath test result due to a discovery violation. The same holds true where the prosecution fails to disclose the most recent record of calibration for the breath test device that was used on your client. For a chemical breath test device result to be admissible, the people must lay a proper foundation that includes the certifications of calibration for the breath test device, certifications of the simulator solution, as well as weekly tests of the simulator solution. *See generally People v. Donaldson*, 319 N.Y.S.2d 172 (1971). In *People v. Corley*, 507 N.Y.S.2d 491 (1986), the Supreme Court Appellate Division reversed a defendant's conviction on two counts of operating a motor vehicle while under the influence of alcohol due to the fact that the people failed to turn over discovery documents relating to the testing and calibration of the breath test device that was used to determine the defendant's blood-alcohol content. In *Corley*, prior to trial, the defense submitted a demand to produce specifically requesting any written reports or documents concerning any scientific tests or experiments relating to the criminal action. The prosecution never produced the requested documents. When defense counsel was supplied with those requested documents at trial, he moved to suppress the breath test results, or alternatively, requested a continuance. The trial court in *Corley* determined that the demand to produce would not be interpreted as a demand for such documentation, and the court denied the motion and the trial ensued, resulting in a guilty verdict. Significantly, the Appellate Division in *Corley* reversed the conviction and agreed with the defendant that there was prejudice due to the people's failure to timely produce documentation, as the breath test maintenance records amounted to written reports or documents concerning a scientific test relating to the criminal action. The court noted that the prosecution's failure to turn over those documents cannot be deemed harmless error, as the admissibility of the breath test result was dependent on the prosecution establishing evidence from which the trier of fact could reasonably conclude that the breath test device was in proper working order at the time the breath test was administered.

Attached as Appendix E is a sample trial memorandum of law that seeks to preclude a breath test device. Attached as Appendix F is a sample cross-examination of a breath test operator.

10

Blood Tests

DUI cases that involve blood tests can be a challenging experience for an attorney defending a DUI case. Many attorneys are fearful of blood cases, as they have little or no experience in litigating cases with blood tests. The reason for this is that blood samples are seldom taken from a defendant. Typically, breath samples are taken. Usually, the only time a blood test is taken is when an individual has been involved in an accident resulting in serious physical injury or death to another person. The only other time blood is usually taken is when a defendant has an accident and has been injured and is taken to a hospital.

The following are suggested areas for the defense attorney to cover in the trial of a DUI blood case.

The Blood Draw

When an individual is under arrest for DUI and a blood sample is to be taken, the first aspect of the blood draw is the cleansing of the draw site.

To cleanse the draw site of a suspect, "an aqueous solution of a nonvolatile antiseptic shall be used on the skin. Alcohol or phenol shall not be used as a skin antiseptic." 10 New York Codes, Rules and Regulations 59.2(d) (10 NYCRR 59.2(d). Typically, a betadine-based solution is used to cleanse the draw site. The solution comes in the standard blood draw kits issued to police officers.

Individuals Authorized to Draw Blood

Pursuant to NY VEH & TRAF § 1194(4), the following are authorized to draw blood:

1. Physician
2. Registered professional nurse
3. Registered physician assistant
4. Certified nurse practitioner
5. Advanced emergency medical technician as certified by the Department of Health; or
6. Under the supervision and at the direction of a physician, registered physician assistant, or certified nurse practitioner acting within his or her lawful scope of practice, or upon the express consent of the person eighteen years of age or older from whom such blood is to be withdrawn: a clinical laboratory technician or clinical laboratory technologist licensed pursuant to the Education Law; a phlebotomist; or a medical laboratory technician or medical technologist employed by a clinical laboratory approved under the Public Health Law.

10 NYCRR 59.2 (c)(l)(i)-V).

The law in New York State previously only allowed physicians to supervise the withdrawing of blood by designated technicians for the purpose of conducting a blood alcohol/drug test. However, recently amended NY PUB HEALTH § 3703(2) now authorizes registered physician assistants and nurse practitioners to also supervise and direct the withdrawal of blood for the purpose of determining the alcohol or drug content therein.

Although there is no requirement under 10 NYCRR 59.2 that the container holding the blood contain a preservative, most often the prosecution's toxicologist will testify that there was one present. Most police blood kits claim to contain a solid anticoagulant consisting of potassium oxalate as well as a preservative consisting of sodium fluoride. Although the manufacturers of the blood kit list on the container that those items are present in each test tube, counsel should object to that listing coming into evidence as hearsay. Also, State Police laboratories do not test for the presence of either a preservative or anticoagulant.

The significance of a preservative added to the blood is great. If no preservative is added to the blood, the blood immediately begins to degrade and can form bacteria that turns into alcohol. This process is called neo-alcohol fermentation, and the result is ethyl alcohol. Significantly, virtually every toxicologist will concede that any neo-alcohol fermentation created will be added to the alcohol that is present at the time of the blood draw. Moreover, there is no way for the toxicologist to determine what percentage of the alcohol was created due to the blood degrading and what percentage of the alcohol was present at the time of the draw. This issue has great significance when you have a case where the blood is not stored in a refrigerated environment for some period of time. If the issue of the blood not being properly refrigerated comes up, most toxicologists will confirm that the process of neo-alcohol fermentation can occur if the blood is stored in non-refrigerated environments for a significant period of time. There have been occasions where blood is kept in police evidence lockers for weeks before its transfer to the lab for analysis. Once it is brought to the lab, it is refrigerated and most all government toxicologists will concede that the blood in the lab is stored in a refrigerated environment to prevent fermentation.

Chain of Custody

Before a blood test result is introduced, a witness or witnesses must be able to identify the evidence as the sample collected from the defendant and that the chain of custody has not been broken. The way this is accomplished is that once the blood is drawn and placed in a vial that is labeled, the vial is then sealed and placed back into the box and then the box is labeled and sealed with tape with the arresting officer's initials on the seal.

Analysis of the Blood

Most laboratories use gas chromatography. The most typical type of analysis is done through headspace gas chromatography.

Headspace gas chromatography is not a direct measurement of blood, but rather an indirect method of measuring the amount of ethanol contained in the liquid by measuring the amount of alcohol in the headspace above the liquid. This returns us to Henry's Law, which was previously described in the materials on breath testing. This issue has great significance when you have a case where the blood is not stored in a refrigerated environment for some period of time. If the issue of the blood not being properly refrigerated comes up, most toxicologists will confirm that the process of neo-alcohol fermentation can occur if the blood is stored in non-refrigerated environments for a significant period of time. There have been occasions where blood is kept in police evidence lockers for weeks before its transfer to the lab for analysis. Once it is brought to the lab, it is refrigerated, and most all government toxicologists will concede that the blood in the lab is stored in a refrigerated environment to prevent fermentation.

In general terms, how headspace gas chromatography works is that blood is prepared in a headspace vial and is mixed with a specific known amount of an internal standard, which is typically some type of alcohol. The laboratory that is conducting the exams will normally create that standard and run tests on the standard to verify the correct amounts. The vial is sealed and ultimately heated to a specific temperature to release the volatile compounds. As the vial continues to be heated, a gas will arise above the mixture and the headspace. The toxicologist will then measure the number of molecules in the headspace and then by conversion quantify the amount of alcohol in the blood below it by using the principles of Henry's Law. That is, because the internal standard of a known amount is mixed into the sample, it will move into the headspace at a known rate. Thus, the alcohol molecules are measured proportionately in relation to the internal standard molecules that are sent into the headspace.

By cross-examining the toxicologist that this is not a direct measurement of blood but rather an indirect measurement, you can ultimately make arguments to the fact finder that this is no better than a standard breath test. The only difference is the gas chromatography is specific for ethanol, while any type of breath test machine is not.

When defending a DUI blood test case, counsel should make similar discovery demands as in breath test cases relative to the calibration and maintenance records of the device used to measure your client's blood. In addition, a demand should be made for copies of all of the controls that are ultimately used as a reference standard in which to measure the blood sample as well as copies of all graphs. Once again, if the prosecution fails to comply with their discovery obligations, you can move to preclude the blood test result as you would to preclude a breath test result due to the failure of the prosecution to comply with your discovery demands.

The above materials are just a very brief overview with regard to defending a DUI blood test case. Anyone who is representing an individual who is charged with DUI where there is a blood test used should consult with authoritative books as well as consult with an expert witness to help understand all physiological and scientific aspects of blood testing. Included as Appendix G is a cross-examination from a blood test case.

11

Trial Order Dismissal and the Necessity of Making the Motion

Upon the completion of the prosecution's case, counsel should make a trial order of dismissal to seek a dismissal of the charges. This motion will almost always be denied, because the evidence must be viewed in the light most favorable to the prosecution. The legal standard when determining this motion is whether the prosecution has established a *prima facia* case by establishing all the elements of the DUI charge. Failure to raise this motion may eventually preclude further appellate review as to whether there was legally sufficient evidence in the case.

The Defense Case

Deciding Whether to Present a Defense

In a DUI case, perhaps more than any other case, often a practitioner will not present a defense by calling any witnesses. The reason for this is that counsel has already attacked the government's case through cross-examination of the prosecution witnesses, trying to establish flaws in their opinion that the defendant was intoxicated in addition to attacking the reliability of the chemical test result. Sometimes, when a defense is presented, and in particular the defendant testifies, the jury is asked to make credibility determinations as to who is more credible, the police witnesses or the accused. When that happens, sometimes the prosecutor will try to argue that the defense is arguing that the police are making up their testimony. That does not mean the defendant should not testify in any case, but rather counsel needs to be prepared to argue to the jury during closing arguments that there is a difference between an officer being mistaken and an officer lying.

Defendant as Witness

The decision whether to testify in a trial belongs to the defendant. In the event that the defendant elects to testify, it is essential to adequately prepare him or her for testimony. If the defendant testifies, he or she should not be argumentative with the prosecutor. The defendant needs to answer all questions honestly and should never answer a question falsely. If there are facts that are going to be established that are harmful to defendant's case, he or she will need to acknowledge those facts as opposed to denying the existence of them. Many times, it is a non-credible answer about an insignificant fact that undermines a defendant's entire credibility. A defendant should also not offer anything more than what is asked and keep his or her answer responsive solely to the question that is asked.

Other Defense Witnesses

In the event that other witnesses testify, the same rules that apply to the defendant also apply to other defense witnesses. They need to be candid, not argumentative, and maintain good eye contact with the jury or the court. In the event that any of those witnesses have any relationship with the defendant, such interest must be brought out on direct examination as opposed to the prosecutor bringing it out during cross-examination. These witnesses also need to be prepared in advance of their testimony. It is essential for a defense attorney to determine what non-defendant witnesses will be called to testify. Typically, non-defendant witnesses will be witnesses who were in a position to have observed the defendant prior to driving or at the time of driving in order to testify that the defendant was not in an intoxicated or impaired condition. Also, if your client was released on his or her own recognizance from the police department to a spouse, relative, or friend, that witness will then be an excellent witness to testify as to your client's condition at the time of his or her release, which is usually shortly after the chemical test. Law enforcement will not release an accused drunk driver to an intoxicated person, so therefore that witness will be credible at least as to not being under the influence of alcohol so that his or her perceptions of the defendant's condition and recollection of his or her condition will be clear.

If you are also fighting the issue of your client's blood-alcohol content or condition of intoxication and/or impairment, you may want to consider trying to establish a timeline defense by calling witnesses who were in your client's presence from earlier in the day up through and after his or her arrest and release. This way you will be able to account for your client's condition for a large period of time and, in so doing, attack the reliability of the officer's opinion that your client was intoxicated as well as attack the reliability of the alleged blood-alcohol content.

Expert Witnesses

Sometimes in DUI trials, expert witnesses will be called by the defense. Typically, these expert witnesses are in the form of toxicologists, pharmacologists, or other experts trying to estimate the defendant's blood-alcohol content at the time of operation and/or attempting to impeach the reliability of the chemical test result.

When choosing an expert, be certain to thoroughly check the expert's qualifications as well as experience in testifying in court on prior occasions.

Remember, the prosecution will typically try to impeach the expert witness by maintaining that they are getting paid for their testimony in the matter. It is important to understand that an expert witness is not being paid for their testimony, but rather is being compensated for the time they are spending on the case. That time includes their prior time consulting with the defense, their time preparing for their trial testimony, as well as their time in court.

The Importance of Preparation

The importance of preparation cannot be overvalued. This includes having a private investigator interview these potential witnesses and having them give a statement shortly after your client's arrest so the prosecution will not be able to argue that the witness is now just coming forward to help a friend. Also, counsel should be aware of his or her own state's evidentiary rules that deal with when it is permissible to impeach a witness with his or her pre-trial silence in not coming forward to law enforcement prior to trial with the exculpatory evidence.

For example, in New York State, since a civilian witness does not have any obligation to come forward with exculpatory information, the prosecution cannot ask a witness about or comment on a witness's failure to come forward unless: (1) the witness is aware that charges were pending and knew to whom the information should be made available (law enforcement), and (2) by such witness's relationship with the defendant, it would have been reasonable for that witness to come forward to the appropriate authorities with such information. *See People v. Dawson*, 50 NY2d 311 (1980). As such, it is imperative for the practitioner to check his or her own state's evidentiary rules to prevent such impeachment evidence.

12

Summations

The summation is that portion of the trial when the attorney gives his or her closing argument by commenting on the evidence and all reasonable inferences that can be drawn from the evidence. An attorney should always give a summation. The following is an example of a hypothetical closing argument:

> To members of the jury:
>
> This will be my last opportunity to speak with you. Initially, my client, Mary Walters, and I both would like to thank you for your jury service and for the attention you have given all participants in this matter. Over the course of my closing remarks, I am going to be commenting on what the evidence has established and why your verdict should be not guilty.
>
> We know that Mary consumed alcoholic beverages prior to operating her motor vehicle. We also know that consuming alcoholic beverages and operating a motor vehicle is not against the law. As Judge Jones will instruct you, it is only against the law if you operate a motor vehicle while under the influence of alcohol, and the judge will define what it means to be under the influence of alcohol. The prosecution has failed to prove to you beyond a reasonable doubt that my client was operating a motor vehicle while under the influence of alcohol.

When examining all of the evidence and applying the law as instructed by Judge Jones, you will be left with many questions. Those questions will not be imaginary; those questions will be real, actual questions as to what happened the night that my client was arrested. Ladies and gentlemen of the jury, those questions will be real, actual reasonable doubts, and as a result of having those doubts, you will not be persuaded beyond a reasonable doubt that Mary is guilty, and therefore you must return a verdict of not guilty.

We know from the evidence that Mary only had two glasses of wine over a two and a half hour period. We know that from the credit card receipt, and we know that from her two work colleagues who were with her and watched her consume those two glasses of wine over the two and a half hour period.

We also know from the evidence that my client was not operating a motor vehicle in any type of erratic fashion that is typically exhibited when an individual is under the influence of alcohol. Rather, Mary was stopped for speeding. Yet, she was maintaining proper control in the steering of her car. The prosecution will ask you to consider my client's performance on the field sobriety tests as an indication that she was intoxicated. I would submit to you, members of the jury, that those field sobriety tests were nothing more than field exercises on a busy highway in the dark of night that consisted of unnatural acts the officer was using to determine what Mary's natural motor coordination skills were. Notably, the officer testified that Mary exhibited no impaired fine motor coordination when she retrieved her license and registration from her wallet and handed it to the trooper. Notably, the trooper did not notice anything unusual about the manner in which Mary exited her vehicle. In fact, he testified that she walked to the back of her car in a normal fashion. Once she got back to the rear of her vehicle in front of the trooper car, that is when she was asked to perform these unnatural physical acts. Now when you get right down to it, the trooper testified on both direct and cross-examination that Mary did not satisfactorily complete the walk-and-turn test because she did not successfully complete the test as instructed and he observed her exhibiting three clues that constituted an unsatisfactory performance. But I respectfully submit to you, members of the jury, that when you break down that walk-and-turn test into the number of actual tasks my client had to do, you will recall that she took nine steps out and nine steps back. Of those total eighteen steps, she missed touching heel-to-toe on two steps out and one step back. Members of the jury, by my calculations, she completed fifteen out of the eighteen tasks correctly with regard to the actual steps taken. Fifteen out of eighteen amounts to 83 percent.

The trooper also indicated that my client exhibited another clue by raising her arms more than six inches from her side between the second and third step on the way out and the fourth and fifth step on the way back. That means that for sixteen out of eighteen steps she took, her arms were in proper position. Members of the jury, that constitutes nearly 89 percent accuracy. And finally, with regard to the walk-and-turn test, the trooper testified that he deducted a point for her because she didn't touch completely heel-to-toe. You may recall, however, that when the trooper was cross-examined, he indicated that he did not recall how much she missed her heel-to-toe by, and he conceded that if missing heel-to-toe was by one-half inch or less, it cannot be counted as a clue for which my client can be penalized. Other than that, my client took the correct number of steps, she properly turned, she counted out loud, she did not begin the test before she was told to begin, and she kept her feet in a heel-to-toe position during the instructional stage. When all of those tasks are added up, Mary performed with over an 85 percent success rate.

The same holds true relative to the one-leg stand test. Calculating all the tasks my client did correctly and comparing them against how many tasks she did incorrectly will also reveal that she completed that with better than 80 percent accuracy. And mind you, ladies and gentlemen, when I'm here standing speaking with you and when the prosecutor gets up to give her closing remarks following mine, take notice whether either one of us are standing on one leg as we are speaking to you. Obviously, I'm not, and obviously, the prosecutor will not be, nor has anyone been doing that while standing during this trial. Once again, the prosecution wants you to find that my client was intoxicated because she was allegedly unable to perform unnatural acts to assess her natural motor coordination skills. I respectfully submit that these are not fair tests to determine whether my client was exhibiting proper motor coordination skills on the evening of her arrest.

Lastly, with regard to the field sobriety tests consisting of the finger-to-nose, my client brought the correct finger of the correct hand and touched her nose. Whether it was the exact tip or slightly above or below the tip, I suggest to you it is not indicative of either passing or failing. Notably, my client was not swaying even though her head was back and her eyes were closed, nor did the officer have to stand in close proximity to her due to any type of fear on his part that Mary would fall and possibly injure herself. Therefore, members of the jury, when you go back into the jury room and deliberate, remember the examples we spoke about during jury selection regarding the difference between a person's subjective opinion and objective facts. I suggest that the arresting trooper's subjective opinions were misplaced and misguided based upon his interpretation of these unnatural physical tasks he was requiring my client to perform, and as such, you are left with reasonable doubts that Mary was intoxicated on the evening of her arrest.

Now with regard to the chemical test result, you heard a lot of testimony from the arresting trooper regarding this breath test device. Notably, the trooper testified that he is not an expert in the device, he can't tell you really how it works, he can't tell you any real details as to the technology behind it, but only that he is trained to operate it.

However, on cross-examination the trooper conceded that there are certain principles at work here such that the breath test device is an indirect measure of an individual's blood alcohol by measuring the amount of alcohol that is in a person's deep lung air and multiplying it by a certain number to get the correlation between the amount of alcohol in blood compared to the amount of alcohol in the lungs. Now, just as the trooper testified that he was not an expert in the breath test device, neither am I, and I suspect, ladies and gentlemen, neither are you. That does not, however, mean that any one of us should blindly accept the test result as the prosecutor is going to ask you to do. Now we learned that this device has a built-in margin of error of plus or minus 0.01 of 1 percent. That is a 20 percent swing margin or error. We also know that it only tells you, assuming everything was working 100 percent accurately, what my client's blood alcohol was purported to be as measured by this machine at the time of the test, which was approximately an hour and fifteen minutes after she was driving. More importantly, my client is accused of having a blood-alcohol content of 0.14 of 1 percent. That is a significant reading. The trooper told you that is more than one and a half times our state's legal limit of 0.08. However, going back to my client's demeanor, her ability to logically and coherently speak and articulate her words to the trooper, her ability to perform the sobriety tests, does it really seem that she was more than one and a half times the state legal limit? Of course it doesn't. Of course it doesn't!

What went wrong with this test? I don't know, and I don't have to prove to you what went wrong. Toasters aren't supposed to burn toast, but sometimes they do. The evidence demonstrates, and all reasonable inferences that can be drawn from the evidence demonstrate, that the tests cannot be reliable.

As the arresting trooper testified, the type of technology used in the breath test device measures a breath sample by looking for a specific concentration of ethanol, which is a type of alcohol in intoxicating beverages. But what the trooper also testified to is that in his training he learned that there are numerous compounds in exhaled human air, and that the breath test device is just not specific for ethanol. That is, other compounds can be contained on a human breath that can be picked up and read as ethanol even though they are not. Once again, the defendant has no burden of proof to establish anything, but we have demonstrated through the prosecution's own witnesses that there are questions or doubts about the accuracy of this breath test and how the breath test works, and those doubts are actual and real reasonable doubts to which my client is entitled.

In just a moment, I will be sitting down and will not be heard from for the rest of this case. I will not be able to stand up and respond to what the prosecutor says in her closing arguments, because that is how our system of law works. The prosecution has the final word. That does not mean, however, that you should not intelligently analyze and question and probe the evidence, and if you do as I have suggested you do, we are confident that you will be left with many questions and doubts as to the condition of Mary on the night of her arrest, as well as to the accuracy and reliability of the chemical test result. And because of those questions and doubts, we are asking you to return a not guilty verdict on the two counts of driving while intoxicated. Thank you.

13

The Sentence

In the event that your client is convicted upon a plea of guilty, you often know either what the precise sentence will be or a sentencing range the court has committed to, including the maximum limit to which the court has indicated it will sentence your client. Nevertheless, the sentencing is when the judge actually, for the first time, will be able to understand what your client's background is and what led him or her to engage in the conduct for which he or she is convicted. This is particularly true if the conviction is after a verdict of guilty and there have not been any extensive plea bargaining discussions prior to trial when the judge may have been made aware of your client's background and the circumstances of his or her arrest.

In many jurisdictions, the county Probation Department will do a pre-sentence investigative report, which is a detailed history of your client's life including family history, educational history, mental and physical health history, employment history, and criminal history. A defendant is often entitled to submit his or her own pre-sentence memorandum in support of his or her sentencing position as well. NY CRIM PRO § 390.40. A defendant's pre-sentence memorandum is an opportunity to put his or her best foot forward in a positive light in order to persuade the judge for a favorable sentence.

Counsel should consider getting character references from people who have known the defendant for a significant period of time. This can include letters from family, friends, former teachers, employers, and anybody else who knows your client.

Having the Client Evaluated by an Alcohol/Substance Abuse Counselor

The importance of having your client evaluated by an alcohol/substance abuse counselor cannot be ignored. Most judges want to have confidence in their decision to not incarcerate your client. Such support can be found in your client accepting responsibility for his or her actions by obtaining an evaluation from a counselor to determine whether your client has an underlying issue with alcohol or chemical dependence. If your client chooses to be evaluated, it is imperative that he or she be completely honest with the evaluator so the counselor can have a workable treatment plan in place in the event that such is determined to be necessary.

The most common fear of any type of prosecutor or judge in a DUI case is that if the individual is not treated severely enough in the criminal justice system, he or she may be at risk to re-offend and a re-offense may involve a drinking and driving-related accident involving a fatality or serious injuries to other individuals. By having your client evaluated by a certified alcohol and substance abuse counselor, and if treatment is required, your client will gain insight as to the issues in his or her life that have led to this type of behavior, and the counselor will have a treatment program in place to help prevent the conduct from reoccurring.

The Defendant's Statement in Court

At the time of sentence, the defendant is also entitled to make a statement to the court. The defendant should be contrite, accept responsibility, and acknowledge the fact that he or she has a problem if in fact a problem exists relative to their use of alcohol or other chemical substances. Counsel must emphasize to their clients that many times what a client states at the time of sentencing can impact the judge in a positive manner so as to obtain a more favorable sentence. Counsel should always know in advance what the defendant is going to state to the court in order to make certain that the information presented to the court will be presented in the best possible light so as to provide the greatest chance of obtaining the most minimal sentence.

14

The Attorney's Role Post-Conviction

The Defendant's Right to Appeal

A defendant has an absolute right to appeal from a conviction and sentence thereon, and from any intermediate order made therein unless the defendant has waived his or her right to appeal. *See People v. Seaberg*, 74 NY2d 1 (1989).

Determining whether to appeal will depend upon each case and the unique facts and circumstances attendant with each case. Counsel will have to assess whether there is a viable appeal based upon an analysis of what happened in the court proceedings and whether there is a viable basis to appeal any prior determination.

Requirement of Filing a Written Notice of Appeal

You will be required to file a written notice of appeal if an appeal is taken. You must check your own state laws to determine when the appeal has to be taken. In New York State, an appeal must be taken within thirty days of a sentence imposed. If you are appealing a denial of a motion to suppress evidence, you must determine from checking your state laws whether an interlocutory appeal by the defense is permitted. In New York State, the defense does not have a right to an interlocutory appeal from a denial of a suppression motion. Rather, there must be a final adjudication (judgment of conviction and sentence thereon), and then an appeal can be taken from any intermediate order previously entered, including an order denying suppression.

If your client is uncertain as to whether he or she wants to appeal, the best practice is to file a *pro se* notice of appeal on behalf of your client so as to protect the client's interests so he or she preserves the right to have appellate review of his or her case.

Issues to Consider in Determining Whether to Take an Appeal

A variety of issues must be considered in determining whether to appeal. Initially, you need to determine whether your client waived his or her right to appeal as part of a plea bargaining agreement. Another issue that needs to be considered in determining whether to appeal is whether any claims that might serve as a basis for an appeal have been waived due to a guilty plea. For example, such claims could be: a statutory speedy trial violation, a claim that the prosecution failed to turn over discovery material such as a prior written or recorded statement of a witness who testified at a pre-trial hearing or trial, or a claim that the evidence presented to the grand jury resulting in the filing of an indictment was insufficient. *See People v. O'Brien*, 56 NY2d 1009 (1982); *People v. Sebastian*, 604 N.Y.S.2d 771 (1993); and *People v. Thomas*, 428 N.Y.S.2d 20 (1980) aff'd 53 NY2d 338 (1981).

In addition, a possible appellate issue may be waived if not properly preserved in the proceedings, such as evidentiary issues for which no objections were raised.

If counsel is not experienced in doing criminal appellate work, he or she should refer his or her client to an attorney who has experience in handling criminal appeals.

APPENDICES

APPENDIX A

SAMPLE RETAINER AGREEMENT

LARKIN, AXELROD, INGRASSIA & TETENBAUM, L.L.P.

RETAINER AGREEMENT

Re: People v.

Our File Number:

1. On this date, I have retained and employed the law firm of Larkin, Axelrod, Ingrassia & Tetenbaum, L.L.P. (hereinafter the "Firm"), to act as my attorneys in the following matter:

2. This agreement does not include representation for any appeals or any post conviction remedies. Such representation requires the payment of an additional retainer and execution of a separate retainer agreement.

3. I agree to pay the Firm the following fees in connection with such services:

A flat fee of $_____________ with an additional $________ per day for hearings and/or trial. For any felony charge(s), the trial fee will be due prior to the commencement of the trial.

There will be an additional flat fee of $_______________ due prior to the Firm appearing in County Court on an Indictment or a Superior Court Information.

In determining the appropriate fee the following factors have been considered: (1) the time and effort required for effective representation, including cerebral aspects in evaluating the case; (2) the responsibility assumed by the Firm in accepting the case; (3) the complexity of the issues involved in the case; (4) the skill and experience required to provide proper and effective representation; (5) the possibility that other employment will be precluded or declined due to any actual or potential conflict of interest issue(s), and due to the time and Firm resources that will be devoted to the case; (6) the gravity of the charges; (7) the experience, reputation, and ability of the attorneys of the Firm; (8) the nature and extent of collateral consequences that must be addressed and/or considered; (9) the amount of time necessary to address the clients needs and concerns; (10) the client's expectations; and (11) the urgency of the matter.

The flat fee does not include any fines, restitution, court costs, court surcharges, or other costs resulting from any sentence. All such are costs for which client solely is responsible.

4. I agree to pay the Firm in addition to the fee stated above, the one-time processing fee of $95.00 per criminal matter. This fee will be used toward postage, telephone calls, photocopying and fax communications.

5. If the entire fee is not prepaid with the signing of this Agreement, then I agree to make the following payments to be applied toward such fee:

Payment of $ on the signing of this Agreement.

Payment of the balance as follows: $_________________ on or before ____________.

If the retainer is being paid in part or in whole by a party other than the client, the client herein specifically agrees and consents to said third party contributing to the payment of said legal fees. Only the person listed above is the client of the Firm, no other person or organization is or will be considered the client of the Firm in this matter. Payor(s) acknowledges, agrees, and understands that they do not and will not have any right to interfere with, direct, or question the professional judgment or legal services provided to client, and the Firm only may disclose/release any information about client's case to any third party with the client's explicit permission. This Agreement is a binding contract, and once signed only the client may discharge the Firm.

6. This agreement is considered a promissory note as it reflects a promise on the client's part to pay the Firm monies owed in accordance with this agreement and is enforceable in any court, tribunal, board or arbitration proceeding. Such note is payable upon demand if the due date for payment has passed and no payment has been made. If a dispute arises regarding attorneys fees paid or owed, the client and the Firm hereby stipulate that the Laws of the State of New York shall be controlling in the interpretation of this contract, and the client and the Firm further stipulate that Orange County, New York shall be the venue for any lawsuit or claim arising out of the interpretation or enforcement of this agreement.

7. I agree that my failure to make any of the payments I have agreed to make herein should be considered as my act of discharging the Firm as my attorneys.

8. I consent, therefore, that the Firm may withdraw as my attorneys after I have failed to make any required payment.

9. You may have the right to arbitration of any fee dispute, pursuant to the rules of the Chief Administrator of the Courts. If a fee dispute arises, and this firm is discharged prior to the completion of the case, this firm will be compensated at an hourly rate of $375.00 per hour for time expended on the file for a partner, $300.00 per hour for time expended by any other associate of the Firm, and $125 per hour for any work performed by a legal assistant or paralegal of the Firm, which would be applied against the initial retainer. Any unearned portion of the retainer will be refunded within thirty (30) business days of the demand of the refund. The $95.00 administration fee is not refundable. If the case is handled by the Firm through the client being sentenced or granted an Adjournment in Contemplation of Dismissal, the client and/or Payor shall not be entitled to a refund of any monies paid to the Firm. Client and Firm agree that any dispute arising out of this Agreement shall be subject to the following: (1) this Agreement shall be interpreted by New York Law, and (2) the venue for any lawsuit, arbitration, or mediation arising out of the interpretation or enforcement of this Agreement shall be Orange County, New York.

10. In addition to the fee set forth above, I agree to pay to the Firm any and all disbursements incurred by them in connection with the subject proceedings. Disbursements include, but are not limited to the following: fees for private investigators, photographs and videotapes relevant to the case, expert witness fees, stenographer appearance fees, transcript fees, Department of Motor Vehicle driving abstract fees, traveling and lodging fees if the case is more than 50 miles from Newburgh, New York. Prior to retaining any private investigator or expert witness, Larkin, Axelrod, Ingrassia & Tetenbaum, L.L.P., will obtain client's oral or written permission for retaining such investigator or expert.

11. I understand that the payment of this Retainer is to retain the Firm and as such the client agrees and consents to have any attorney representative of the Firm to represent the defendant herein. Nothing contained herein shall be construed to mean that any particular attorney or attorneys of the Firm shall be designated or obligated to do any or all work or appear in Court on the matter for which the Firm is being retained.

12. I understand that the Firm will rely upon my promises in this Retainer Agreement, and I understand that these promises are the consideration given to the Firm to obtain their services.

13. The Firm does not warrant, guarantee, or promise any specific outcome or result with regard to our representation in this case.

14. In the event that an appearance is scheduled for a violation of probation, a violation of a conditional discharge or a restoration of an Adjournment in Contemplation of Dismissal (ACD), there must be a separate written Retainer Agreement executed by the client and the Firm reflecting the fees and terms of retention in order for the Firm to appear in court for any such violation or restoration. In addition, a separate retainer and the execution of a new Retainer Agreement will be required for any applications to modify a condition of any sentence, including but not limited to modifying terms and/or conditions or probation, applying to a court for a Certificate of Relief from Disabilities, or applying to a court or to the Department of Motor Vehicles for reinstatement of driving privileges.

15. Neither Client, nor the Firm shall record any oral communications between Client and the Firm. If Client records any oral communication with the Firm, Client forfeits all monies paid to the Firm under this Agreement, and by signing this Agreement, Client expressly consents to allow the Firm to withdraw as counsel in the above-referenced case if Client records any such communication.

16. Client expressly agrees and understands that it is a waiver of the attorney/client privilege between Client and the Firm if the Firm or any employee of the Firm is grieved or sued by Client , if the Firm is required to sue Client to enforce the terms or conditions of this Agreement, if Client breaches any material provision of the Agreement so as to mandate a motion to withdraw, or if in the course of disparagement of the Firm or any member of the Firm Client discloses any fact which would otherwise be privileged.

17. This document represents the entire agreement and terms of representation between the Firm and the retaining party. No term or condition can be modified unless it is done in writing and signed by all parties.

18. I have read each and every paragraph of this Retainer Agreement and accept the terms and conditions contained herein.

DATED: , 2011

ACCEPTED AND AGREED:

____
BY:

LARKIN, AXELROD, INGRASSIA
& TETENBAUM, L.L.P.

BY:___________________________

STATEMENT OF CLIENT'S RIGHTS AND RESPONSIBILITIES

Your attorney is providing you with this document to inform you of what you, as a client, are entitled to by law or by custom. To help prevent any misunderstanding between you and your attorney please read this document carefully.

If you ever have any questions about these rights, or about the way your case is being handled, do not hesitate to ask your attorney. He or she should be readily available to represent your best interests and keep you informed about your case.

An attorney may not refuse to represent you on the basis of race, creed, color, sex, sexual orientation, age, national origin or disability.

You are entitled to an attorney who will be capable of handling your case; show you courtesy and consideration at all times; represent you zealously; and preserve your confidences and secrets that are revealed in the course of the relationship.

You are entitled to a written retainer agreement which must set forth, in plain language, the nature of the relationship and the details of the fee arrangement. At your request, and before you sign the agreement, you are entitled to have your attorney clarify in writing any of its terms, or include additional provisions.

You are entitled to fully understand the proposed rates and retainer fee before you sign a retainer agreement, as in any other contract.

You may refuse to enter into any fee arrangement that you find unsatisfactory.

Your attorney may not request a fee that is contingent on the securing of a divorce or on the amount of money or property that may be obtained.

Your attorney may not request a retainer fee that is nonrefundable. That is, should you discharge your attorney withdraw from the case, before the retainer is used up, he or she is entitled to be paid commensurate with the work performed on your case and any expenses, but must return the balance of the retainer to you. However, your attorney may enter into a minimum fee arrangement with you that provides for the payment of a specific amount below which the fee will not fall based upon the handling of the cases to its conclusion.

You are entitled to know the approximate number of attorneys and other legal staff members who will be working on your case at any given time and what you will charged for the services of each.

You are entitled to know in advance how you will be asked to pay legal fees and expenses, and how the retainer, if any, will be spent.

At your request, and after your attorney has had a reasonable opportunity to investigate your case, you are entitled to be given an estimate of approximate future costs of your case, which estimate shall be made in good faith but may be subject to change due to facts and circumstances affecting the case.

You are entitled to receive a written, itemized bill on a regular basis, at least every 60 days.

You are expected to review the itemized bills sent by counsel, and to raise any objections or errors in a timely manner. Time spent in discussion or explanation of bills will not be charged to you.

You are expected to be truthful in all discussions with your attorney, and to provide all relevant information and documentation to enable him or her to competently prepare your case.

You are entitled to be kept informed of the status of your case, and to be provided with copies of correspondence and documents prepared on your behalf or received from the court or your adversary.

You have the right to be present in court at the time that conferences are held.

You are entitled to make the ultimate decision on the objectives to be pursued in your case, and to make the final decision regarding the settlement of your case.

Your attorney's written retainer agreement must specify under what circumstances he or she might seek to withdraw as your attorney for nonpayment of legal fees. If an action or proceeding is pending, the court may give your attorney a "charging lien," which entitles your attorney to payment for services already rendered at the end of the case out of the proceeds of the final order or judgment.

You are under no legal obligation to sign a confession of judgment or promissory note, or to agree to a lien or mortgage on your home to cover legal fees. Your attorney's written retainer agreement must specify whether, and under what circumstances, such security may be requested. In no event may such security interest be obtained by your attorney without prior court approval and notice to your adversary. An attorney's security interest in the marital residence cannot be foreclosed against you.

You are entitled to have your attorney's best effort exerted on your behalf, but no particular results can be guaranteed.

If you entrust money with an attorney for an escrow deposit in your case, the attorney must safeguard the escrow in a special bank account. You are entitled to a written escrow agreement, and may request that one or more interest-bearing bank accounts be used. You are also entitled to a written receipt, and a complete record concerning the escrow. When the terms of the escrow agreement have been performed, the attorney must promptly make payment of the escrow to all persons who are entitled to it.

In the event of a fee dispute, you may have the right to see arbitration. You attorney will provide you with the necessary information regarding arbitration in the event of a fee dispute, or upon your request.

Receipt Acknowledged:

Dated: , 2011

____

LARKIN, AXELROD, INGRASSIA & TETENBAUM, L.L.P.

____

APPENDIX B

SAMPLE DISCOVERY DEMAND

STATE OF NEW YORK : COUNTY OF ORANGE
JUSTICE COURT : TOWN OF

THE PEOPLE OF THE STATE OF NEW YORK,

-against-

NOTICE OF APPEARANCE AND DEMAND FOR SUPPORTING DEPOSITION

Defendant.

SIRS:

PLEASE TAKE NOTICE that the undersigned attorneys appear in the above action as attorney of record for the defendant herein and demand that all papers and pleadings hereinafter served be sent to the undersigned at the address below stated.

PLEASE TAKE FURTHER NOTICE that the undersigned demands that pursuant to the provisions of Section 100.25(2) of the C.P.L., that supporting depositions of the charge against the defendant stated in the accusatory instruments(s) charging: Driving While Intoxicated in violation of Sections 1192(2) and 1192(3), Failed to Stop at a Stop Sign in violation of Section 1172(a) and Drove Across Hazard Markings in violation of Section 1128(d) of the New York Vehicle & Traffic Laws, be served upon the undersigned by , 2011. Said deposition must state thereon which facts alleged therein are upon personal knowledge and which are upon information and belief.

DATED:

Yours, etc.,

LARKIN, AXELROD, INGRASSIA
& TETENBAUM, L.L.P.
Attorneys for Defendant
356 Meadow Avenue
Newburgh, NY 12550
(845) 566-5345

STATE OF NEW YORK : COUNTY OF ORANGE
JUSTICE COURT : TOWN OF

THE PEOPLE OF THE STATE OF NEW YORK,

-against- **DEMAND TO PRODUCE**

Defendant.

SIRS:

PLEASE TAKE NOTICE that the defendant, through her attorneys, LARKIN, AXELROD, INGRASSIA & TETENBAUM, L.L.P., pursuant to Article 240 of the Criminal Procedure Law, hereby demands discovery of the following designated property by , 2011:

1. Any written, recorded, or oral statement of the defendant made other than in the course of the criminal transaction to a public servant engaged in law enforcement activity or to a person then acting under her direction or in cooperation with her, including, but not limited to, statements at the police headquarters.

2. Any written report or document, or portion thereof, concerning a physical or mental examination or scientific test or experiment relating to the criminal action or proceeding and made by, or at the direction of a public servant engaged in law enforcement activity.

3. Any photographs, diagrams, or drawings relating to the criminal action or proceeding made or completed by a public servant engaged in law enforcement.

4. Any photographs, videotapes or electronic recordings which the prosecution is in possession of relating to the criminal action regardless of whether the prosecution intends to introduce same into evidence.

5. Any other property obtained from the defendant.

6. Any tapes or other electronic records which the prosecution intends to introduce at the trial.

7. The names and criminal records of the People's witnesses.

8. Any and all statements of the People's witnesses made to a public servant engaged in law enforcement activity or to a person then acting under her direction or in cooperation with her.

9. The names and criminal records of individuals who have given statements to a public servant engaged in law enforcement activity or to a person then acting under her direction or in cooperation with her.

10. The conflicts among the accounts given by different prosecution witnesses or by a single witness in separate reports, notes, or accounts.

11. The exact time of the defendant's arrest and the time which any blood tests were performed.

12. Any evidence tending to effect the credibility of the People's witnesses.

13. Any promises made to any of the People's witnesses by the District Attorney's Office or by a public servant engaged in law enforcement activity or by a person then acting under her direction or in cooperation with her.

14. The links in the chain of physical evidence that are missing or non-existent.

15. All records, memoranda, logs, writings, and reports concerning the defendant's date, time and place of arrest, her being taken into custody, her entry into the police building and her subsequent release.

16. The instrument, including model number, employed to determine the alcoholic content of the defendant's blood.

17. All tests performed to determine the alcoholic content of the defendant's blood level and under what circumstances such tests were made and who was present.

18. To make available to the defendant any ampoules, as well as the original air sample taken from the defendant, the original reference sample, and the disposable sanitary mouthpiece or saliva trap used in the testing of the defendant.

19. A complete set of engineering drawings, plans and specifications of the instrument used to test the alcoholic content of the defendant's breath on the day the incident occurred.

20. The serial number and date of manufacture, together with the date of delivery, to the department of the instrument unit in question.

21. The full corporate name and address of the manufacturer of the unit in question.

22. Copies of all printed or written tests and research data submitted by the manufacturer of the instrument to any Federal, State or local agency or government unit.

23. The variable of the degree of error with the machine in question.

24. Any and all precautionary checklists used by the operators of the instrument in question.

25. All data of similar kind now in possession of any agency as set forth above which is in the possession or under the control of said agency, but which was neither

independently gathered by said agency or submitted by parties other than the manufacturer of the instrument.

26. A copy of the complete maintenance history of the instrument in question.

27. The complete test of copies of any directive notice or bulletin, or item of similar type, as issued to the using agencies by and of the above manufacturers of the instrument involved.

28. A copy of the instruction manual as supplied with the particular instrument in question, together with copies of each other instruction manual that has been supplied by the manufacturer of the machine or by governmental agency involved prior to or subsequent to the issuance of the manual as delivered together with the machine.

29. The results of all supporting data related thereto now in possession or under the control of any government agency as mentioned above herein of any comparative tests between the unit in question and any other breath testing machine.

30. The results of each and every breath test as run on the unit now in possession of the department for the last year.

31. To allow the defendant's attorneys and defendant's expert witnesses access to the unit in question now in the pos-session of the department upon giving of a reasonable notice for the purpose of examining and testing said machine as against the plans and specifications as set out by the manufacturer. Said inspection to be carried out in a manner and fashion consistent with the integrity of such evidence at a time and place which is mutually agreeable to the defendant, her expert and the People.

32. Any and all certificates of calibration for the instrument employed to determine the alcoholic content of the defendant's blood for the preceding year.

33. Any and all certifications for the simulator solution for the six months preceding the defendant's arrest up to the present.

34. Copies of the weekly tests run on the simulator solution the machine employed to determine the alcoholic content of the defendant's blood for six months preceding the defendant's arrest up to the present.

35. Copies of all the department rules of the arresting agency governing the utilization of the breathalyzer instrument.

36. A copy of the operations permit, if any, of the police officer who administered the blood alcohol test to the defendant.

37. Any and all certificates for the ampoules, or their lot numbers, which were used in this matter.

38. The evidence or information creating a reasonable doubt as to the

defendant's guilt.

39. Anything else required to be disclosed prior to trial to the defendant by the People, pursuant to the Constitution of the State and of the United States.

DATED:

Yours, etc.,

LARKIN, AXELROD, INGRASSIA
& TETENBAUM, L.L.P.
356 Meadow Avenue
Newburgh, NY 12550
(845) 566-5345

STATE OF NEW YORK : COUNTY OF ORANGE
JUSTICE COURT : TOWN OF

THE PEOPLE OF THE STATE OF NEW YORK,

-against-

DEMAND FOR A BILL OF PARTICULARS

Defendant.

SIRS:

PLEASE TAKE NOTICE, that the defendant, through her attorneys, LARKIN, AXELROD, INGRASSIA & TETENBAUM, L.L.P., requests the District Attorney's Office to file and serve a Bill of Particulars with the following necessary information:

1. The exact date, time and location of the alleged offense, making specific mention of land marks and/or reference points as to the location.

2. The exact time and location the defendant was first observed by the arresting officer, making specific mention of landmarks and/or reference points as to the location.

3. The exact date, time and place of the defendant's arrest.

4. An exact description of the defendant's conduct which is alleged to have constituted the offense charged, and the names and addresses of the persons alleged to have witnessed said conduct.

5. The names and addresses of the People's witnesses.

6. If the People intend to offer scientific evidence, then the defendant demands the exact date, time and location such analysis was performed, together with the results of said analysis.

7. If the People intend to offer such scientific evidence, the defendant demands the name and address of the person or persons who performed such analysis and the names and addresses of any witnesses to such analysis.

8. If the People intend to offer such scientific evidence, then the defendant demands a statement of whether it is alleged that the consent for such analysis was voluntarily given by the defendant.

9. Whether the People intend to offer any physical evidence against the defendant, and if the answer is yes, then whether it is alleged that the defendant had possession of said physical evidence.

10. Whether the People have utilized any tape or other recording or photographic devices in the conduct of the investigation of this case.

11. Whether the People intend to offer or use any evidence of the defendant's prior crimes, bad conduct or bad acts, and if the answer is yes, then the defendant moves for an account of such evidence together with a copy of her New York State and Federal Criminal History Summary Sheets.

DATED:

Yours, etc.,

LARKIN, AXELROD, INGRASSIA
& TETENBAUM, L.L.P.
Attorneys for Defendant
356 Meadow Avenue
Newburgh, NY 12550
(845) 566-5345

APPENDIX C

SAMPLE DWI MOTION

STATE OF NEW YORK : COUNTY OF ORANGE
JUSTICE COURT : TOWN OF
- x
THE PEOPLE OF THE STATE OF NEW YORK

-against- **NOTICE OF MOTION**

Defendant.
- x
SIRS:

PLEASE TAKE NOTICE that upon the annexed affirmation of JOHN INGRASSIA, an associate of the law firm of LARKIN, AXELROD, INGRASSIA & TETENBAUM, L.L.P., attorneys for the defendant, and upon all the pleadings and proceedings heretofore had herein, a motion will be made at a regular term of this Court on the day of , 2011 at o'clock in the afternoon of that day, or as soon thereafter as counsel may be heard, for the following relief:

A. For an order for a bill of particulars pursuant to CPL Section 200.90;
B. For an order of preclusion pursuant to CPL Section 240.20, CPL Section 240.40, and CPL Section 240.70;
C. For an order for disclosure pursuant to Brady v Maryland;
D. For an order suppressing any and all confessions or admissions or, in the alternative, for a pre-trial hearing;
E. For an order suppressing the breath test results or, in the alternative, for a pre-trial hearing; and
F. For an order for disclosure pursuant to People v. Geaslen;
G. For an order for a pre-trial hearing pursuant to People v Sandoval;
H. For an order for a pre-trial hearing pursuant to People v. Ventimiglia;

As to each of the above requests, for such other and further relief as to this Court may seem just and proper.

Dated: Newburgh, New York

Yours, etc.
LARKIN, AXELROD, INGRASSIA
& TETENBAUM, L.L.P.
Attorneys for Defendant
356 Meadow Avenue
Newburgh, NY 12550
Tel. (845) 566-5345

STATE OF NEW YORK : COUNTY OF ORANGE
JUSTICE COURT : TOWN OF

- x

THE PEOPLE OF THE STATE OF NEW YORK

-against-

SUPPORTING AFFIRMATION

Defendant.

- x

JOHN INGRASSIA, ESQ., an attorney admitted to practice law in the Courts of the State of New York, affirms the following under the penalties of perjury:

1. That I am a member of the law firm of Larkin, Axelrod, Ingrassia & Tetenbaum, L.L.P., the attorneys for the above-named defendant, and am fully familiar with the facts, pleadings, and circumstances of the above-captioned matter.

2. That I make this affirmation in support of the application now before this Court. Any statement made herein is based upon information and belief the source of such information and grounds for such belief being a review of the case file maintained by our office and independent investigations.

A. AS TO THE DEFENDANT'S MOTION FOR A BILL OF PARTICULARS

3. Adequate preparation is essential in the defense of anyone charged with any offense. The material requested in the following motion for a Bill of Particulars is relevant and necessary in order for the defendant and your deponent to properly prepare for trial and to avoid undue and unfair surprise at the trial of the above-captioned matter. Upon information and belief, all of the requested information is within the control of the District Attorney.

4. Therefore, your deponent respectfully requests that the Court direct the District Attorney to file and serve a Bill of Particulars with the necessary following information:

a. The exact date, time, and location of the alleged offense, making specific mention of landmarks and/or reference points as to the location.

b. The exact time and location the defendant was first observed by the arresting officer, making specific mention of the landmarks and/or reference points as to the location.

c. The exact date, time, and place of defendant's arrest.

d. An exact description of the defendant's conduct which is alleged to have constituted the offense charged, and the names and addresses of the persons alleged to have witnessed the said conduct.

e. The names and addresses of the People's witnesses.

f. The name and address of the manufacturer of the instrument used in the above-captioned matter to measure defendant's blood alcohol level.

g. The type, and serial and model number of the instrument used in the above-captioned matter.

h. The name of the instrument's operator, the date of his original certification, the date of this latest certification, and the date of all simulator tests run by him within 12 months prior to the giving of the defendant's test.

i. Whether the instrument has been tested for Radio Frequency Interference (RFI) and if so, the dates of the testing, the circumstances under which the testing was done, the person who tested the instrument, the RFI sources the instrument was subjected to, and the distance each source was to the instrument.

j. The timing device used to determine the time of the test, whether it has been certified, and if so, proof of the certification.

k. Assuming that the instrument was inspected, serviced, checked for accuracy, and certified in proper working order, the dates and names of the operator or certification officer who did this just prior to and after the test was administered to defendant, the time of the first test and result, the time of the second test and result.

l. Whether anyone in the police agency read to defendant her Miranda rights or breathalyzer warnings, if so, who did it, how many times were they read, where were they read to defendant, when were they read to her, and what was defendant's response to same.

m. Whether defendant requested an attorney, if so, at what time, whether defendant was allowed an opportunity to make a telephone call, if so, when, to whom, and for what purpose.

n. Whether a sample of defendant's breath, blood, or urine was obtained by the police agency, if so, whether it was preserved, tested or destroyed.

o. Whether any physical condition tests were performed, if so, the type used, the results, who conducted them, the time and the exact location of said tests.

p. Whether an alco-sensor test was administered, if so, the model number, make, and serial number of the instrument, the degree of permissible variance, the readings, the time and exact location variance, the readings, the time and exact location given. Whether the alco-sensor was ever inspected, tested, serviced or checked for accuracy, if so, the name of the operator, the date of the testing, and the results of the testing.

q. If blood or urine testing was done, identify:

(l) the testing method used;
(2) the qualifications of the person who performed the test;
(3) the date, time, and place of the test;
(4) whether the test was performed using enzymatic analysis, color-metric distillation, alcohol separations, or any other procedure;
(5) whether any preservatives, anticoagulants, or other reagents were added to the blood or and, if so, the name of the preservative, anticoagulant, or reagent, the amount added, by whom it was added, and the time it was added;
(6) a complete list of all persons in the chain of custody and possession of the blood or urine sample.

r. Whether defendant at any time indicated a desire to take any other chemical test pursuant to Section 1194(8) of the Vehicle and Traffic law of the State of New York, and if so, indicate:

(l) to whom the statement was made to;
(2) what additional tests were taken;
(3) who defendant indicated he wished to administer the test;
(4) whether defendant was afforded that opportunity, and;
(5) what the result of said test was.

s. Whether the People have utilized any tape, video tape, photographs or any other recordings, and if so, identify:

(l) the name of the person who took the photographs or acted as technician for sound or video recordings;
(2) the time the photographs, sound or video recordings were taken;
(3) the present location of any photographs, sound or video recordings;
(4) the location at which they were taken;
(5) the circumstances under which they were taken;
(6) the technical experience of the person who took the photographs or who acted as technician for the sound or video recordings;
(7) whether defendant was given an opportunity to refuse to have her

picture taken, or be subjected to sound or video recordings, and if so, what was said to defendant concerning her right to refuse; and

(8) whether defendant was read her Miranda rights or any other rights prior to the taking of the photographs, sound or video recordings.

t. Whether the People intend to offer any physical evidence against the defendant, and if the answer is yes, then whether it is alleged that the defendant had possession of said physical evidence.

u. Whether the People intend to use or offer any evidence of defendant's prior crimes, bad conduct or bad acts, and if the answer is yes, then the defendant moves for an account of such evidence together with a copy of her New York State and Federal Criminal History Sheets.

B. AS TO THE DEFENDANT'S MOTION FOR AN ORDER OF DISCOVERY

5. "The criminal discovery procedure embodied in Article 240...evinces a legislative determination that the trial of a criminal charge should not be a sporting event where each side remains ignorant of facts in the hands of the adversary until events unfold at trial" (People v Copicotto, 50 NY2d 222, 226 (1980); People v Minor, 118 Misc.2d 351, 352 (N.Y.Co.Ct., 1983)).

6. Broader pre-trial discovery enables the defendant to make a more informed plea decision, minimize the tactical and unfair advantage to one side, and increase the opportunity for an accurate determination of guilt or innocence (Copicotto, supra at 226; Minor, supra at 352). Discovery by the defense contributes substantially to the fair and effective administration of justice (Copicotto, supra at 226; Minor, supra at 352).

7. If a party does not comply with these liberalized discovery proceedings Criminal Procedure Law Section 240.70(l) provides: The Courts may order such party to permit discovery of the property not previously disclosed, grant a continuance, issue a protective order, prohibit the introduction of certain evidence or the calling of certain witnesses or take other appropriate actions.

In determining whether a preclusion remedy should be granted, the trial Court should also take into account that the purpose of Criminal Procedure Law Article 240 was to broaden pre-trial discovery (see People v Thomas, 106 Misc. 2d 64, 67 (N.Y.City. Crim Ct 1980); see also People v Brown, 104 Misc. 2d 157, 164 (N.Y.City. Crim Ct 1980).

8. A Demand to Produce was served on the District Attorney. The District Attorney has responded incorrectly and inadequately to the Demand. The failure to answer or move in any manner with respect to the Demand, authorizes the Court to impose the sanctions set forth in Article 240 of the CPL. That the appropriate sanction to impose is to preclude the People from introducing any evidence encompassed by the Demand. If the Court feels that the sanctions are not appropriate, the Defendant respectfully moves this Court for an order directing the Discovery and Inspection of the following lettered list. This motion is made in the firm belief that such items are material and necessary to the preparation of her defense since the items of discovery and inspection requested are solely in the control and possession of the District Attorney and otherwise unobtainable by the defendant and very important to the proper and adequate preparation of the defense so that the defendant may receive a fair trial which is not fraught with surprise and unfair advantage inasmuch as basic fairness and simple practicality dictate that the People are not disadvantaged by such disclosure because the People's evidence does not change with the degree of disclosure the District Attorney is directed to make.

i. The names of the People's witnesses. The disclosure of names of potential witnesses in proper. Such a request should be granted absent a showing that there are compelling circumstances to indicate that potential witnesses would be tampered with or threatened. People v Barnes, 74 Misc. 2d 743 (N.Y.Co.Ct.1973); People v Cohen, 60 Misc. 2d 706 (Sup. Ct. Richmond Cnty.1969); People v Harrison, 81 Misc. 2d 144 (Just. Ct. Town Chenango 1975). "The right of a defendant to discover a potentially material witness must be balanced against a **found** fear that such a disclosure might lead to the intimidation of the witness or the influencing of his testimony. However, with the proper safeguards, if the evidence is of material to the defense on the questions of guilt or innocence, it should be disclosed." People v Andre W, 44 NY2d l79 (1978) (emphasis added). Due to the particular nature of this particular case, the information is material and important to the defendant's case. In addition, such disclosure will enable counsel to avoid undue surprise, adequately cross examine witness, and avoid unnecessary delays. If the Court denies this part of the defendant's motion, we would ask that the Court order the People to disclose the requested information sufficiently in advance of the scheduled trial date so as to enable the defendant to properly prepare for trial.

ii. What links in the chain of physical evidence are missing or non-existent.

iii. The instrument, including model number, employed to determine the alcoholic content of the defendant's blood.

iv. The variable degree of error for the machine in question.

v. What evidence or information creates a reasonable doubt as to the defendant's guilt.

vi. All records, memoranda, logs, writings and reports concerning the defendant's date, time and place of arrest, her being taken into custody, her entry into the police station, and her subsequent release.

vii. If the People intend to offer or introduce any physical evidence against the defendant, then the defendant moves to examine or have her expert examine such evidence at least twenty (20) days prior to trial and in a manner and fashion consistent with the integrity of the evidence and at a time and place where it is mutually agreeable to the defendant, her expert and the District Attorney.

viii. Copies of the handwritten notes and reports competed and/or filed by the People's witnesses in connection with this case, together with copies of any accident report filed in connection with this case.

ix. Any and all certificates of calibration for the instrument employed to determine the alcoholic content of the defendant's blood for the preceding year.

x. Any and all certificates for the simulator solution for the six months preceding the defendant's arrest up to the present.

xi. Copies of the weekly tests run on the simulator solution the machine employed to determine the alcoholic content of the defendant's blood for the six month preceding the defendant's arrest up to the present.

xii. Copies of all the department rules of the arresting agency governing the utilization of the breathalyzer instrument.

xiii. A copy of any written departmental policy or guidelines outlining and/or mandating either required or suggested materials for administration of field tests, and/or documenting and/or judging the results thereof.

xiv. A copy of the operator's permit, if any, of the police officer who administered the blood alcohol test to the defendant.

xv. Any and all certificates for ampoules, or their lot numbers, which were used in this matter.

xvi. What evidence or information creates a reasonable doubt as to the defendant's guilt.

xvii. Any records of repair made on the instrument within the past year.

xviii. A portion of the sample of the breath, saliva, urine, blood taken from the defendant by the police agency.

xix. If any field tests were performed, state and describe the exact nature of each such test.

xx. The results of any field tests which were performed for sobriety and/or intoxication upon or by the defendant.

xxi. Copies of any and all reports of scientific tests upon which the People intend to rely and/or introduce at trial.

xxii. The criminal records of any witnesses the People intend to call at trial.

xxiii. The defense demands an opportunity to examine any and all photographs and/or physical evidence which the People intend to introduce at trial, or which were used or taken in connection with this case.

xxiv. Copies of the criminal records of the defendant, if any, so that the defense can determine the necessity of a motion pursuant to People v Sandoval, 34 NY2d, 371 (1974).

xxv. Any evidence and/or information now in the possession of the prosecution, their agents, including but not limited to the police agencies involved in this matter which is favorable to the defense.

xxvi. Copies of any and all inventories of properties seized from the defendant by the police, prosecution or their agents or about the time of defendant's arrest.

xxvii. The name and address of any persons who are alleged to have participated with the defendant in the crimes alleged.

xxiii. Copies of any and all inventories of property seized from the defendant by the police agencies and other agents of the prosecution, at or about the time of defendant's arrest.

xxix. If any such tests were performed by means of any machine or instrument, as previously set forth herein, the defense requests an opportunity to inspect and evaluate such instrument or machine.

xxx. If a breathalyzer test was performed set forth a copy of the rules and regulations of the police agency which own or maintains said instrument governing its use and operation.

xxxi. If a breathalyzer instrument was used in this case, set forth a copy of the Certificate of Calibration records for said instrument for one year prior to this arrest and for the period from the arrest to the present, along with the simulator test record of tests for the same periods to give defense an opportunity to inspect said records prior to trial. Also set forth a copy of Record of Analysis of Breath Analyzer Ampoules for the ampoules used in testing of this defendant and a copy of instrument in question prior to or subsequent to the test of this defendant.

xxxii. If a breathalyzer instrument was used in this case, set forth a true and exact copy of the New York State Health Department Certificate certifying that said operator is currently approved to perform such tests.

xxxiii. State whether any tests for the Radio Frequency Interference have been performed on the instrument utilized in this case.

xxxiv. If so, state specifically whether tests were performed for background Radio Frequency Interference, for base station transmission Radio Frequency Interference and for mobile and handheld transmitter Radio Frequency Interference on the instrument utilized in this case. If such tests were performed, state by whom said tests were performed and the results of said tests, as well as the date and place of the performance of said tests.

xxxv. Any written reports or documents concerning a physical or mental examination or scientific test or experiment relating to the criminal action made by or at direction of a public servant engaged in law enforcement activity.

C. AS TO THE DEFENDANT'S MOTION FOR DISCOVERY OF BRADY MATERIAL

9. Because the Courts have, through their interpretation of the Constitution of the United States and the State of New York, placed a continuing obligation upon the Prosecutor to disclose to the defendant all the evidence bearing on her innocence as well as evidence which is exculpatory in nature and aids in her defense, the defendant respectfully requests the Court to order disclosure of the following information:

a) If a machine was used to determine the defendant's blood alcohol content, describe or identify the following:

(I) type of machine used;
(2) manufacturer of machine;
(3) date of manufacture;
(4) date of purchase by agency or department

making the tests;
(5) number of prior tests made on the machine;
(6) all maintenance on the machine in last two years;
(7) all calibrations on the machine in the last two years;

b) If chemicals were used to determine the defendant's blood alcohol content, describe or identify the following:

(l) all chemicals used, by name and chemical composition;
(2) supplier of chemicals;
(3) date of purchase;
(4) place where chemicals are stored;
(5) all persons who have access to stored chemicals;
(6) all methods and procedures used in preparation of chemicals for test, including but not limited to mixing and diluting of chemicals.

c) With respect to the person who administered a test to determine the defendant's blood alcohol content, describe or identify the following:

(l) name of person administering the test;
(2) department or agency by whom such person is employed;
(3) compliance with the statutes and regulations as to standards of training for persons administering and interpreting chemical tests for intoxication.

d) With respect to the person, if any, who interpreted the test to determine the defendant's blood alcohol concentration, describe or identify the following:

(l) name of person interpreting the test;
(2) department or agency by whom such person is employed;
(3) compliance with the statutes and regulations as to standards of training for the persons administering and interpreting chemical tests for intoxication.

e) If a breathalyzer was used to determine the defendant's blood alcohol content, describe or identify the following:

(l) the model number and manufacturer;
(2) any testing conducted by the police agency for Radio Frequency Interference;
(3) if testing was done for Radio Frequency

Testing, provide the date, and time and manner of such testing, who conducted such tests, and the results thereof.

f) If a blood sample was taken and used to determine the defendant's blood alcohol content, describe or identify:

(l) the person taking such sample;
(2) the manner, time, date, and location the sample was taken;
(3) whether the person taking said blood sample cleansed the area of skin from which the sample was taken with any alcohol based solution.

D. AS TO THE DEFENDANT'S MOTION FOR AN ORDER SUPPRESSING EVIDENCE OF ANY OF THE DEFENDANT'S STATEMENTS, OR IN THE ALTERNATIVE, AN ORDER FOR PRE-TRIAL HEARINGS

10. The District Attorney has served the defendant with a notice indicating his intent to offer testimony at her trial concerning the defendant's alleged confession or admission. Defendant only moves for suppression of those statements for which the People have served a timely CPL 710.30 notice. Defendant moves to preclude all other statements if any, which defendant has not received timely CPL 710.30 notice.

11. The defendant was arrested and charged with having committed certain offenses.

12. The defendant has discussed the circumstances of her arrest and processing with her attorney. Knowledge of the defendant's rights at the time of and after her arrest have been discussed. Furthermore, the defendant's education and mental and physical condition at the time of her arrest have been discussed.

13. Any statements allegedly made were in violation of the defendant's right to counsel and, therefore, should be suppressed.

14. Upon information and belief, that any such statements claimed to have been made were made by means of promises, or statements of fact which created a substantial risk that the defendant might falsely incriminate herself.

15. Upon information and belief, that any such statements claimed to have been made

were made in violation of the defendant's New York and United States Constitutional rights, to include that the defendant was not advised and/or did not appreciate her right to remain silent, her right to talk to a lawyer or to have a lawyer present, or the fact that what was said would be used against her or the fact that if he could not afford to hire an attorney, one would be appointed at no cost to her.

16. Upon information and belief, that any such statements claimed to have been made were made at a time when there was no probable cause to believe that the defendant had committed any crime.

17. Since all facts that surround the making of any claimed statements are not completely known to the defendant, and are known to the People, the defendant is unable to claim any more than previously stated of any other specific constitutional or other violations. If the Court determines that because of the defendant's lack of knowledge of specific facts, the Court is unable to order the suppression of such claimed evidence based on the present affidavit, then the defendant respectfully submits that the Court, in protecting constitutional rights, should order an evidentiary hearing prior to trial.

E. AS TO THE DEFENDANT'S MOTION FOR AN ORDER SUPPRESSING THE RESULTS OF THE CHEMICAL TESTS

18. The defendant further moves pursuant to CPL Section 710.20(1) for the suppression of any and all evidence gained as a result of the defendant's warrantless arrest since the same was gathered in violation of her rights under the Constitution of the United States as well as the State of New York. Specifically, it is asserted that any and all evidence gained as a result of the defendant's arrest, both direct and indirect, must be suppressed since the police officers did not have probable cause to believe that the defendant was operating a motor vehicle while under the influence of alcohol.

19. Particularly, in this case, the defendant was arrested by the police officer as

indicated in uniform traffic tickets that were issued. As a result of this arrest, the defendant was taken into police headquarters and was directed to submit to a chemical test. Thus, as a result of such test, certain physical and tangible evidence was seized from the defendant, to wit: her breath, and the defendant further has reasonable cause to believe that said evidence would be introduced at the trial herein.

20. It is respectfully submitted that such evidence must be suppressed together with the fruits thereof, both direct and indirect, because they consist of tangible property obtained by the means of an unlawful search and seizure under circumstances precluding the admissibility thereof in criminal action against the defendant. In support of this motion, your deponent submits the following allegations of fact which are based upon information and belief. The source of said information and the grounds for said belief consist of conversations your deponent has had with the defendant, and personal investigation into this matter, and independent investigation of the document submitted herein, particularly the information sworn to by the arresting police officer, as well as a review of the relevant law in this area.

21. In the present case, it is respectfully submitted that the defendant was arrested on the charge of Driving While Intoxicated in the absence of reasonable cause to believe that she indeed was operating a motor vehicle while under the influence of alcohol. Defendant was operating her vehicle in compliance with all State and local laws. The defendant's vehicle was not being operated in an erratic fashion. After being unlawfully stopped, defendant's speech was clear and logically responsive to questions asked of her. Defendant was steady on her feet and adequately performed the field sobriety tests asked of her by following the instructions and completing the required tasks. During her encounter with police, defendant was not exhibiting impaired motor coordination consistent with being under the influence of alcohol.

22. Specifically, it is uncontroverted in the present case that the defendant was

arrested without an arrest warrant for violating Section 1192 of the Vehicle and Traffic Law. However, such an arrest is authorized pursuant to CPL Section 140.10(1)(a) only when:

> "(the police officer) has reasonable cause to
> believe that such a person has committed such offense
> in his presence..."

23. Moreover, since no arrest warrant was issued, the People have an affirmative burden of establishing the legality of the warrantless seizure of the defendant's person (People v Pepitone, 48 AD2d 135, 368 NYS2d 181, 183 (1st Dept. 1975) aff'd, 39 NY2d 907, NYS2d 401 (1976); People v Berrios, 28 NY2d 361, 367, 321, NYS2d 884, 889 (1971). Such a showing requires, at the minimum that the police officer must establish a good faith belief which rests firmly upon "specific and articulable facts" (Terry v Ohio, 392 U.S. 1 (1968); People v Sobotker, 43 NY2d 599, 565, 402, NYS2d 993, 996, (1978); People v Ingle, 36 NY2d 413, 369, NYS2d 67, 72 (1975) which are sufficient in themselves to induce a reasonably prudent and cautious man to believe that the person arrested has committed the **offense being charged** (People v Cantor, 36 NY2d 106, 103, 365, NYS2d 519, 516 (1975); People v Martin , 33 NY2d 123, 124, 343, NYS2d 343, 345, (1973).

24. Moreover, in order to constitute reasonable cause to justify the seizure of the defendant, facts relied upon by the police officers must be capable of measurement against an objective standard. See, Delaware v Prouse, 99 S. Ct. 1391, 1397 (1979).

25. In the present case, it is submitted that the People cannot meet the heavy burden of establishing reasonable cause for the arrest of the defendant. Specifically, based upon your deponent's review of the pleadings herein, it is submitted that the People cannot establish that the defendant was intoxicated **prior to her arrest** nor did the arresting officers otherwise have probable cause for the seizure of the defendant. Thus, since the initial seizure of the defendant was unlawful, any and all evidence derived therefrom must be suppressed as "fruit"

of the primary illegality (Wong Sun v United States, 371, U.S. 471, 484, (1963), including, but not limited to, any and all observations made of the defendant by the arresting officers as well as the breathalyzer test administered herein.

26. Furthermore, since the law is well settled that any warrantless search and seizure is, **per se**, unreasonable and thus unconstitutional, the heavy burden rests upon the People to demonstrate by clear and convincing evidence that one of the carefully delineated exceptions to the warrant clause exists. See People v Baker, 23 NY2d 319, 321, 296, NYS2d 745, 752, (1968); People v Mahoney, 16 AD2d 107, 400, NYS2d 257, 258 (4th Dept., 1977). In the present case, it is submitted that the People will rely upon the exception purportedly contained in the Vehicle and Traffic Law Section 1194 in the form of implied consent.

27. However, in order to come within the exception created by the Vehicle and Traffic Law Section 1194, the procedures and requirements set forth therein **must be** strictly adhered to. Specifically, Section 1194-1(1) provides for an implied consent to the administration of a chemical test of a person's blood only if the police officers have "reasonable grounds to believe such person to be driving in violation of...section eleven hundred and ninety-two..."

28. In addition, since there was no probable cause for the defendant's arrest, the search and seizure cannot stand on the grounds of being incident to a valid arrest in that there was no probable cause for the arrest, and thus, the absolute prerequisite for search incident to arrest does not exist. See, People v Mailinsky, 15 NY2d 86, 91, 262 NYS2d 65, 79 (1965).

29. Moreover, based upon my conversation with the defendant, there was no valid, lawful, voluntary and informed consent to said search and seizure of the defendant's person nor her breath.

30. Thus, it is respectfully submitted that since the prerequisites for administration of the breathalyzer pursuant to Section 1194 of the Vehicle and Traffic Law have to been met, the

results of the chemical test administered must be suppressed. In the alternative, since the law is well settled that the burden is upon the People to go forward in the first instance with clear and convincing evidence in support of the legality of any warrantless search and seizures, at the very least, the defendant is entitled to a hearing in which the People must produce evidence justifying the search and seizure conducted in this case.

31. That upon information and belief, the defendant did not consent to the taking of the breath sample, that prior to taking the breath sample, the defendant was not properly advised of this right to counsel and of her right to refuse to submit to the breath test pursuant to statute.

32. That the said test was not, upon information and belief, taken within two (2) hours of defendant's arrest.

33. That upon information and belief, the person who took the sample from defendant was not qualified or authorized to so by statute (1194(l7), V.T.L.) or by the NYCRR.

34. Therefore, the defendant respectfully requests that the evidence herein be suppressed in all respects because it was seized without a warrant or probable cause, it was not incident to a lawful or valid arrest, it was not taken within two (2) hours of defendant's arrest, the person who took the evidence was not qualified or authorized to do so; nor was it conducted pursuant to a valid consent on the part of the defendant. Moreover, the search and seizure which led to the discovery of the evidence which forms the basis for this prosecution was not conducted, it is believed, in accordance with Section 1194 of the Vehicle and Traffic Law. In the alternative, this Court should conduct a suppression hearing, and upon completion thereof, enter an Order suppressing any and all evidence obtained from the defendant, together with the fruits thereof.

F. AS TO THE DEFENDANT'S MOTION FOR AN ORDER FOR DISCLOSURE PURSUANT TO PEOPLE V. GEASLEN

35. Defendant also moves for disclosure of Geaslen material pursuant to People v. Geaslen, 54 N.Y.2d 510 (1981). Pursuant to this authority, defendant moves for disclosure of any and all information which may be favorable to the defendant and thereby might affect the Court's Decision on a suppression issue, in a fashion favorable to the accused.

36. In light of the above, the defendant respectfully requests that the Court order the People to provide the defendant with any and all information indicative that this prosecution is based on and/or is a product of evidence obtained as a result of governmental action which is in violation of the defendant's Constitutional Rights.

G. AS FOR DEFENDANT'S MOTION FOR AN ORDER PURSUANT TO PEOPLE V SANDOVAL AND PURSUANT TO CPL SECTION 240.43 AS TO THE ADMISSIBILITY OF PRIOR ACTS AND UNCHARGED CRIMINAL, VICIOUS, AND IMMORAL ACTS

37. Upon information and belief, the People may attempt to introduce evidence of a prior arrest and alleged prior vicious or criminal conduct of the defendant at the time of her trial.

38. To allow the People to use any purported acts and/or convictions for purposes of impeaching the defendant's credibility would unfairly affect her as a witness on her own behalf. The prejudicial effect of the admission of such evidence for impeachment purposes would so outweigh its probative worth on the issue of credibility as to warrants its execution. Furthermore, the introduction of such evidence may have the effect of discouraging the defendant from testifying on her own behalf.

39. It is, therefore, respectfully requested that this Court preclude the People from examining the defendant with respect to any convictions or prior bad acts.

40. The defendant hereby requests that the District Attorney notify her attorney of all

specific instances of prior uncharged criminal, vicious, or immoral conduct which the prosecutor has knowledge and which the prosecutor intends to use at trial for the purposes of impeaching the defendant's credibility pursuant to Section 240.43 of the Criminal Procedure Law.

H. AS TO THE DEFENDANT'S REQUEST FOR A PRE-TRIAL HEARING PURSUANT TO PEOPLE V VENTIMIGLIA

41. Defendant also moves for a hearing pursuant People v. Ventimiglia, 52 NY2d 350 to determine the admissibility of any prior uncharged criminal, vicious or immoral or bad acts on the part of the defendant. Defendant maintains that if such evidence is introduced the prejudicial effect will substantially outweigh any probative value with regard to the admissibility of such evidence. Accordingly, the defendant respectfully requests that this Court issue an Order precluding the People from introducing such evidence on either its direct case or through the cross-examination of the defendant should he elect to testify or on its rebuttal case. In the alternative, the defendant respectfully requests that the Court conduct a pre-trial hearing to determine the admissibility of same. If the Court does conduct a hearing, the defendant respectfully requests that the Court direct the People to disclose all of the specific instances of prior uncharged criminal, vicious, immoral or bad acts which the People intend to introduce upon the trial of this matter prior to such hearing.

WHEREFORE, your deponent respectfully requests that the relief sought herein be granted together with such other and further relief as the Court may deem just and proper.

Dated: Newburgh, New York

JOHN INGRASSIA

APPENDIX D

SAMPLE CROSS-EXAMINATION OF AN ARRESTING OFFICER

[redacted] - Direct

yes. And how much she was drinking and she stated five to six tequila sunrises. And I asked her where she was drinking and she stated Pineapples in [redacted] with a couple of friends after work.

Q And at any time did you threaten, coerce or promise anything to the defendant in exchange to her speaking to you?

A No.

[redacted]: I have no further questions, Judge.

THE COURT: Okay, Counselor.

CROSS-EXAMINATION

BY MR. INGRASSIA:

Q Good evening, Officer [redacted]. My name is John Ingrassia and I'm an attorney in [redacted] and I represent [redacted] Sir, you indicated that you made two to three dozen arrests for DWI over the course of your career in law enforcement, about four years, correct?

A Approximately.

Q And back on February 20th, 2003 would it be fair to say that you still had made about the same number of arrests, maybe one or more arrests since that date, five months removed from then?

A It's fair to say that.

[redacted] - Cross

Q So is it fair to say then that you are familiar with the paperwork you filled out in your DWI arrest from your department back on February 20th of 2003, correct?

A Okay.

Q And now do you believe that the events of February 20th, 2003 were better in your mind, in your recollection, back when you observed those events on February 20th than they are today on July 9th, 2003?

A Yes.

Q Okay. And obviously you made other arrests and filled out other documents since then, correct?

A Yes, sir.

Q And you filled out a variety of those documents which I referred to as [redacted] material. You heard that [redacted] record, correct?

A Right.

Q And since then you haven't made any type of amendments to any of your reports, have you?

A No.

Q And I am sure that you reviewed them -- do they have to be reviewed by a supervisor?

A Yes.

Q For content and accuracy, correct?

[redacted] - Cross

A Yes.

Q And everything that you filled out is truthful and accurate, correct?

A Yes.

Q And you signed verification that any type of false statements are punishable as a misdemeanor, correct?

A Correct.

Q And your department amended or supplemental reports, correct?

A Yes.

Q And there was no need for you to file anything in that regard, correct?

A No.

Q And you indicated that my client was placed under arrest at 11:25 p.m., correct?

A Correct.

Q And that she was read her Miranda warnings and DWI refusal warnings sometime simultaneously at 11:30 p.m., correct?

A Correct.

Q And that was done at the [redacted] Police Department, correct?

A Yes, correct.

[redacted] - Cross

Q And about how far were you from the [redacted] Police Department from where the accident scene was and the DWI investigation?

A Less than a mile and a half.

Q Okay. Now, at the location of the accident --

A Yes.

Q -- you arrived on the scene, correct?

A Yes.

Q And the first thing that you noticed was a vehicle, yes?

A Yes.

Q And ultimately you learned the identity of my client, [redacted] yes?

A Yes.

Q And she was already out of the vehicle, correct?

A Yes.

Q And you engaged her in certain type of conversation, did you not?

A Yes.

Q Okay. And determined that she was the operator of the vehicle, correct?

A Yes.

Q And that conversation occurred at what time?

[redacted] - Cross

If you need to refer to the 710.30 notice --

A Yes.

Q -- to refresh your recollection, I think that's People's 1 for identification. You just can't read it out loud. Look at that if you need to do that, and please feel free -- the initial conversation, sir, was when?

A 11:25.

Q Okay. And that would be 11:25 on February 21st, correct?

A Yes.

Q Now, where did that conversation take place?

A At the scene.

Q Okay, and outside of my client's vehicle?

A Outside of my patrol vehicle, yes.

Q Okay. And where was your vehicle in relation to Sara's vehicle?

A [redacted] vehicle was facing southbound and I was in the northbound lane.

Q And would you agree with me that there was snow on the road, based on your prior testimony, correct?

A Snow wasn't on the roadway, it was on the --

Q Shoulder area?

A -- shoulder area of the roadway.

[redacted] - Cross

Q And would you agree with me, sir, that the road surface itself was wet?

A Yes.

Q And you noted that in your report, correct?

A Uh-huh.

Q Now, you inquired as to how the accident happened, correct?

A Yes.

Q And she indicated to you in some respect that she was making a call or doing something with her cell phone and essentially took her eyes off the road and lost control of the vehicle, correct?

A Correct.

Q And you know that it's unlawful under the Vehicle and Traffic Law to communicate on the cell phone absent of a hands-free device while you are operating a motor vehicle, correct?

A Correct.

Q And in fact you issued a ticket for that, correct?

A Correct.

Q And you learned in your training and experience that an individual who was talking on the cell phone may have their attention diverted, cause them to lose control

[redacted] - Cross

of their vehicle, correct?

A Yes.

Q Now, you did inquire as to whether or not she was injured, correct?

A Yes.

Q And she indicated that she was not, correct?

A Correct.

Q Did you ever inquire as to whether or not she was feeling ill that evening?

A No.

Q Now, from the sobriety tests that you attest to, I know you couldn't recall the Walk and Turn, correct?

A Correct.

Q You couldn't -- well, you indicated that the One Leg Stand was performed and she didn't get to count to 30 and she put her foot down two times, correct?

A Yes.

Q And I take it from that, sir, you were not able to articulate for Judge [redacted] as to what number or what count she put her foot down, correct?

A No, I can't.

Q Would there be anything, sir, that would refresh your recollection as to what count she put her

[redacted] - Cross

foot down, other than the fact that it was somewhere before number 30?

A No.

Q You made no notes in that regard, correct?

A No.

Q With the sobriety tests done, were the notes made in terms of any reports, pen to paper, pencil to paper, key pad, computer generated back at the station?

A Yes.

Q And that was obviously after the sobriety tests, correct?

A Yes.

Q And where were the sobriety tests completed?

A The sobriety tests were completed on the road side.

Q And did you demonstrate the Walk and Turn test?

A Yes, I demonstrated all the tests.

Q And where were the defendant given, specifically in relation to where [redacted] vehicle was and where your vehicle was?

A [redacted] vehicle was on the opposite side of the roadway facing northbound where my vehicle was where the test was administered, right in front of my police car.

Q And the headlights were on, correct?

[redacted] - Cross

A Yes.

Q Wig-wagging, alternating lights?

A Just the rotating lights.

Q Spotlight, take-down as well?

A No. Spotlight was on her vehicle.

Q Okay.

A Because when I pulled up to the scene of the accident I put the spotlight on her vehicle.

Q So regardless of that then, your headlights were illuminating, lighting the area where she had performed these tests, correct?

A Yes.

Q Now, are you certified, sir, by the National Highway Traffic and Safety Administration relative to the administration of standardized field sobriety tests?

A I am now, yes.

Q And at the time, were you?

A No.

Q Okay. And you learned at some point in time there are three standardized sobriety tests, correct?

A Yes.

Q Two of which you administered, correct?

A Yes.

Q And the other one, the Gaze Nystagmus, you did

[redacted] - Cross

not administer?

A No, because I wasn't certified.

Q Of the two standardized field sobriety tests, the Walk and Turn, you have no recollection of that you can articulate to the Court as to how she performed on that test, correct?

A Correct.

Q And on the One Leg Stand is that she put her foot down two times?

A Yes.

Q Without telling us what numbers, correct?

A Yes.

Q Did you learn or did you specifically instruct Sara during that One Leg Stand test that if she put her foot down she was to continue the test by raising her foot back up, that left -- six inch position and continue to count from where she left off when she put it down? Did you instruct her on that?

A Well, can you just --

Q Sure. Did you receive a blue book such as this (indicating), DWI detection standardized field sobriety testing produced by our federal government, United States Department of Transportation?

A Yes, recently.

[redacted] - Cross

Q And as part of your course, this is your student book, correct?

A Yes. I just took the course.

Q And did you take it locally in the police academy?

A This class I took at the [redacted] Sheriff's Department recently.

Q And you had a standardized field sobriety test instructor who gave you this?

A Yes.

Q And you had to take a written test and a performance test, correct?

A Yes.

Q My question to you, you may recall -- I know you weren't certified at the time of this arrest, but my question to you is, did you ever give her instructions, Sara?

A Okay.

Q And that if she were to put her foot down during this One Legged Stand that she is to pick her foot back up in that six inch position and continue the count from where she left off, so hypothetically if she put her foot down on 12, she is to pick her foot back up, 13, 1000, 14, 1000 -- did you give those instructions to

[redacted] - Cross

her?

A No, I didn't.

Q And as you sit here now, did you learn that a standardized field sobriety test, it's just that, that it's a standardized test, such that a [redacted] office administers it the same way as a City [redacted] office or as a [redacted] State Highway patrol officer or as a [redacted] state trooper?

A Yes.

Q And under the circumstances and conditions that they have to work with, yes?

A Yes.

Q And did you also learn that the instructions had to be precisely followed in order to validate the actual administration of the test as well as to evaluating performance of that test?

A Yes.

Q And did you learn in your training that a subject for the One Leg Stand test, that if a subject puts their foot down and they're allowed to pick it up and continue?

A Yes.

Q But that was not given to [redacted].

A No.

[redacted] - Cross

Q Would you agree with me then, that that test itself -- that the One Legged Stand, that's established by our federal government allows the subject to put his or her foot down as part of that test?

A Yes, it does, give them --

Q And did you learn that one of the criteria of automatic failure is if the subject puts her foot down or his foot down three times?

A Yes.

Q And she did not do that, correct?

A No.

Q And other than putting her foot down two times, and we know that -- you know that it was somewhere between one and 29, correct?

A Yes.

Q There was no other reason why -- there was no other recollection that you have as you sit here this evening, as to why failed that test, correct?

A No.

Q Yet you determined and relied upon your evaluation and interpretation as you knew it at the time to be a failure, correct?

A Yes.

Q And you relied on that, Officer, including that

[redacted] - Cross

she in part was under the influence of alcohol, correct?

A Yes.

Q And did you also learn on -- in your training that the -- what type of footwear was she wearing that evening, do you recall?

A I don't recall.

Q And do you have any -- anything that would refresh your recollection one way or the other?

A No.

Q Whether it was sneakers or sandals?

A I don't recall.

Q Heels or anything like that?

A I don't recall.

Q Sir, did you learn in your training and I realize -- I don't mean to put you on the spot, I realize most of your training happened after this arrest, that it's critically important to determine what type of footwear the subject is wearing, correct?

A Correct.

Q Because if the subject is wearing any shoe with a heel, a heel greater than two inches, the validity of that test is also compromised, correct?

A Correct.

Q Absent them being afforded the opportunity to

[redacted] - Cross

remove that heel, correct?

A Yes.

Q As you sit here today, you cannot tell the judge what shoe she was wearing?

A I do not recall.

Q Or the size of the heel?

A No.

Q Did you also learn in order for that test to be valid, in order for it administered in a standardized situation, it has to be administered on a reasonably dry, not slippery surface, correct?

A Yes.

Q And if something is wet, it cannot be reasonably dry, correct?

A Correct.

Q Yet you weren't aware of that when you characterized her performance as a failure on that One Legged Stand test, correct?

A Correct.

Q Now, you also have no recollection as to that Walk and Turn test, correct?

A No.

Q And would you agree with me that you learned in your training -- and if you need to look at this book,

[redacted] - Cross

let me know, that that Walk and Turn test also had to be administered, to be valid, on a reasonable dry, non-slippery surface?

A Yes.

Q And again, if the road surface is wet, it cannot be reasonably dry, correct?

A Yes.

Q And that test would have been compromised, correct, the validity, correct?

A Correct.

Q Now, the Finger to Nose test is a non-standardized test, correct?

A Correct.

Q Now, you made have received some training in that Finger to Nose test, correct?

A Yes, I did.

Q And did you learn in your training at the Bureau Municipal Police or at the police academy you attended --

A [redacted] Police Academy which I attended.

Q Did you receive -- Well let me withdraw that question. Do you know if the [redacted] Police Department -- and that's who you are affiliated with, correct?

A Yes, sir.

[redacted] - Cross

Q Do they, sir, have any type of standardized criteria relative to the administration of that Finger to Nose test?

A No.

Q Do they have any standardized criteria relative to scoring or evaluation of such a test?

A No, sir.

Q Would you agree with me then, that that test really is subjective in nature, both in terms of administration as well as performance evaluation?

A Yes.

Q And what I mean by that is you have the discretion to administer it one way and if I were an officer I may have the discretion to administer it another way, you know, like the federally standardized sobriety tests, correct?

A Correct.

Q And you indicated to me that there were a variety of different instructions that were given to her, correct?

A Yes.

Q And did you tell her first to stand with her feet together or shoulder width apart?

A Well, for which test?

[redacted] - Cross

Q For the Finger to Nose test?

A Yes.

Q And did you tell her to put her hand initially at her side?

A At her side initially.

Q Correct. And to watch you, correct?

A Yes.

Q And did you tell her then that you were going to orally or verbally instruct her on that test, correct?

A Yes.

Q And you told her that she was to extend both her arms out, correct?

A Correct.

Q And then ultimately put her head back, correct?

A Yes.

Q And close her eyes, correct?

A Yes, sir.

Q And on your command either right or left, she was to bring the right index finger on the right command and touch the tip of her nose with her finger and on the left command touch the tip of her nose with her left index finger, correct?

A Correct.

Q All the while her head is back and eyes closed,

[redacted] - Cross

correct?

A Correct.

Q Now, you indicated that without knowing specifically on each occasion, she missed the tip of her nose, correct?

A Yes.

Q And sometimes she hit above it and sometimes she hit below it?

A Yes, yes.

Q Do you know how many times, she had three on each side?

A It would be three on each side.

Q Usually the protocol is right, left, right, left, left, right?

A Yes.

Q Just like that, right, left, right, left, left, right?

A I do left, right first.

Q So left, right, left right, right, left?

A Left, right, left, right, right, left, yes.

Q Now, you are looking for a variety of clues on that test, correct?

A Correct.

Q All right. And based upon your training and

[redacted] - Cross

experience now, other than her missing her nose with the tips of her finger, tips of her nose with her finger, did you fail her due to any other reasons?

A She was a little unbalanced, wobbly.

Q Now, did you learn that an individual balance is better when they are standing up or when the head is back?

A When they are standing up.

Q Of course, right? Did you learn also that when their head is back and the subject closes their eyes, that their balance is even further affected?

A Yes.

Q And did you learn in your training, especially with the NHTSA that well over 70 to 75 percent of subjects, persons and humans balance comes from their eyes, point of reference, horizon, correct?

A Correct.

Q So when a person has her head back and their balance is already less or poorer, that the correct upright position and they close their eyes then even further, for lack of a better word, magnified or amplified their imbalance, correct?

A Yes.

Q Did you have to catch her?

[redacted] - Cross

A No.

Q Did another officer have to catch her?

A No.

Q Was anybody standing behind her?

A No.

Q So there was nothing that led you to believe that she was in danger of basically falling, hurting --

A No.

Q Did she appear to be nervous during your encounter?

A Yes, she did appear to be nervous the whole time.

Q And that's not uncommon even for a speeding ticket, correct?

A Correct.

Q Have you ever experienced yourself or any other individual in your training or experience who was nervous and who sometimes get a little thick-tongued or slurred speech?

A I -- in my account I've never had anyone who had gotten thick-tongued, maybe wobbly or shaking when they are giving me their driver's license, but --

Q What's the first word that she slurred?

A The first word?

[redacted] - Cross

Q Yes, sir.
A When I asked her if she was driving.
Q And what did she say?
A Yes.
Q And that was it?
A Yes.
Q You were able to understand it?
A I could understand it.
Q Would you say she was cooperative with you?
A Yes, oh, yes.
Q And the information that she provided to you was logically responsive to the questions being asked, correct?
A Correct.
Q And despite the slurred speech you were able to understand what she was physically articulating to you, correct?
A Yes.
Q Now, about how long -- you indicated I think, and please correct me if I am wrong, I don't want to put words in your mouth, when the sergeant was off duty or came on duty or whatever, passed by, you were sort of, kind of trying to take control of the accident scene, flow traffic, et cetera, and he was -- she was seated in

[redacted] - Cross

the patrol car for about how long?

A About 15 minutes I would say.

Q This was before the sobriety test, correct?

A This is just to get her off of the roadway.

Q So she is in the vehicle -- I'm sorry, you have the initial conversation and you determine that she is out of the vehicle and you determine that she is the operator and you start to observe some of this indicia and then you put her in the patrol car and you continue with your duties and then the sobriety testing begins, correct?

A Correct.

Q Now, you learned the importance of filing accurate paperwork, did you not?

A Yes.

Q Okay. Cases even reliability of information, officer safety can rely upon the accuracy of information, correct?

A Correct.

Q And you know everything is accurate in these reports, correct?

A Correct.

Q As well as the accusatory instrument, correct?

A Correct.

[redacted] - Cross

Q Now, it's okay I'm sure you probably discussed this case with the District Attorney at some point earlier this evening or this afternoon in preparation of your testimony, correct?

A Correct.

Q Now, how many traffic tickets did you fill out in this case?

A Three.

Q One of them was for using hand-held cell phone, correct?

A Yes.

Q One of them was for driving while intoxicated, per se, .10 or more?

A Yes.

Q And one was for common law operating while intoxicated, 1192, sub 3, correct?

A Yes.

Q Of the Vehicle and Traffic Law nothing else, correct?

A No, no other traffic tickets, no.

Q So there was nothing in your investigation from your personal investigation or information that you learned from [redacted] that led you to believe that the accident was caused by anything other than driver

[redacted] - Cross

inattention from using a hand-held cell phone?

A Correct.

Q And in fact you did not consider her having had any type of erratic operation, correct?

A Correct.

Q Now, you indicated -- by the way, I apologize if I asked you this question, but had you ever met [redacted] before this date?

A No.

Q So it's fair to say that you don't know her normal manner of speech, correct?

A No.

Q Now, when you were interacting with her, 11:25 at night, correct, when you are having these conversations with her?

A Approximately.

Q And you knew that she was coming from a location that you learned to be a bar in [redacted]?

A A bar, restaurant.

Q And did you learn, other than the five tequilas that she had, did you ever ask her at any point in time what -- what time she first started drinking?

A I think I did, I think I did. It would be on my alcohol influence report.

[redacted] - Cross

Q Do you recall, sir, whether she told you that she had her first drink at 6 p.m. one way or the other? If you need to look at it, just let me know.

A Yes, if I could look at it that would be great.

Q I think that this is two pages, so what I am going to do is borrow the court's stapler and staple it and have this marked as Defendant's A, entitled alcohol influence report form. If I could have the -- I'm showing this to the A.D.A.

(Whereupon, alcohol influence report was marked as Defendant's Exhibit A for identification by the reporter.)

Q Sir, I think probably on the second page I'd ask you to take a look at that and read that to yourself and when you are done reading that I need to ask you a few questions regarding that.

(Whereupon the witness is reviewing Defendant's Exhibit A.)

Q Okay, sir, does that refresh your recollection?

A Yes.

Q As to what time she indicated that she started drinking?

A Yes, sir.

Q And tell the Court?

[redacted] - Cross

A 6 p.m.

Q And can you tell us what time she stopped drinking?

A 10 p.m.

Q She would have had five alcoholic beverages in four hours, correct?

A Correct.

Q And from the time that you had your contact with her and placed her under arrest at 11:25 p.m., we are talking five hours and 25 minutes would have elapsed since her consumption of those five drinks, correct?

A Correct.

Q Now, you also asked her some questions -- maybe I can just come up closer and you may need to look at it, and so will I, I asked her if she was driving the vehicle, correct?

A Correct.

Q And she indicated, yes, correct?

A Yes.

Q And which way was she driving on [redacted], do you know?

A Southbound.

Q Okay. And you asked her where she was going, correct?

[redacted] - Cross

A Yes.

Q And she told you home, correct?

A Yes.

Q And you asked her what highway she was on, correct?

A Uh-huh.

Q And she told you [redacted], correct?

A Yes.

Q And you asked her which direction, south, correct?

A Yes.

Q And the you asked her at some point in time there is an interview process, I realize some of these questions may have been approximations and everything, but what time is it now, correct?

A Yes.

Q And that's part of the influence report interview process, correct?

A Yes.

Q And the answer she gave was 1 a.m., correct? You need to look at it? Sure, okay.

A I need to look at it, yes.

(Whereupon, the witness is reviewing Defendant's Exhibit A.)

[redacted] - Cross

Q And then you asked her what locality she was in and she told you [redacted], correct?

A Yes.

Q And then you asked her what is the date, correct?

A Yes.

Q And she told you the date was 2/21, correct?

A Yes.

Q And it was a Friday, correct.

A Yes.

Q And then there was a spot for you to fill in as well, correct?

A Yes.

Q The actual -- in reality time and dates, correct?

A Yes.

Q And you filled in 1 a.m. consistent with her answer, correct?

A Uh-huh.

Q And it was Friday, February 21st, correct?

A Yes.

Q And would you agree with me that this was filled out within an hour and a half of her arrest, correct?

[redacted] - Cross

A Yes.

Q Within an hour of her breathalyzer test, correct?

A Yes.

Q If you need to refresh your recollection as to the times --

A No, I have it.

Q And the information she provided was accurate, yes?

A Yes.

Q And -- you indicated that she had a strong odor of alcoholic beverage coming from her breath?

A Yes.

Q And did you learn from your training and experience through the National Highway Traffic Safety Administration and standardized field sobriety program that the type of alcohol contained in intoxicating beverages is something known as ethanol, ethanol alcohol?

A Uh-huh.

Q Yes or no?

A Uh-huh, yes.

Q Ethanol is an odorless type of compound, correct?

A Yes.

[redacted] - Cross

Q From the -- since odorless substances from odor alone even a certified field sobriety test individual, and a person who has made two to three dozen arrests, trained officer, is unable to determine from the odor alone, what a person had to drink, correct?

A Correct.

Q And how much a person had to drink, correct?

A Correct.

Q And when a person first consumed, correct?

A Correct.

Q Or when a person last consumed?

A Correct.

Q Somebody consumed some type of alcoholic beverage several hours before, that can still leave a distinct odor, strong odor of an alcoholic beverage on the breath, correct?

A Yes.

Q And would you agree with me then that the consumption or the odor of alcoholic beverage is not an indication in and of itself of an individual being under the influence of alcohol?

A No, it's not.

Q It's just an indication of somebody having consumed alcohol at some point in time in the past?

[redacted] - Cross

A Yes.

Q Now, you indicated that she had glassy eyes as well?

A Yes.

Q And could you describe to the Court what you mean by glassy eyes?

A What do I mean?

Q Yes, sir.

A They were red and when you looked at them they just -- if I was to look at your eyes right now, they are -- her eyes were bloodshot --

Q Bloodshot?

A -- glassy looking, which means they just don't look -- they don't look right.

Q Did you learn in your training and experience it could be a multitude of causes for bloodshot, glassy eyes separate and apart from being under the influence of alcohol?

A Yes.

Q And what are some of those causes that you learned in your experience?

A I don't recall.

Q Fatigue, being tired, that could be one of them?

[redacted] - Cross

A Could be one of them.

Q Having -- sensitive to allergies?

A If you have allergies, I assume so.

Q I don't want you to assume, I just want to know if you learned any of this in your training?

A I didn't learn that, no.

Q Having smoke sensitive from second-hand smoke?

A I don't recall learning those, to be honest with you.

Q Okay. Now, would you agree with me that you did not consider my client -- you were in her presence for about an hour and a half to two hours that evening?

A Approximately.

Q From start to finish. She was released ultimately, correct?

A Yes.

Q Would you agree with me officer that you did not consider or were not of the opinion that my client was exhibiting any type of impaired motor coordination during your encounter with her?

A No.

Q That's true or not true?

A That's true.

Q And in fact you did not check that box on -- in

[redacted] - Cross

Exhibit A?

A Right.

Q And would you agree with me that a classic sign of an individual who is under the influence of alcohol as defined by the New York State Vehicle & Traffic Law to any extent, even impaired, typically, classically exhibits impaired motor coordination?

A Yes.

Q Now, when you went over the DWI warnings, Miranda warnings with her, it was important for you to be certain that [redacted] was aware of all of her constitutional rights, correct?

A Yes.

Q As well as aware of any consequences of any chemical test -- and we do know that she voluntarily submitted to a test, correct?

A Yes.

Q And you were satisfied that she fully understood each and every one of those rights, correct?

A Yes.

Q She didn't question you about that, correct?

A No.

Q And you had her initial portions in which she understood her rights, correct?

[redacted] - Cross

A Yes.

Q And that she did not wish to speak to an attorney, correct?

A Correct.

Q And in fact she never requested to speak to an attorney any time that evening, correct?

A Correct.

Q And you asked her to even write out yes or no in terms of whether or not she would voluntarily submit to a chemical test at the bottom of that form, correct?

A Correct.

Q And she wrote yes, that's her handwriting, correct?

A Yes.

Q And those are her initials, correct?

A Yes.

Q Now, the date was on February 21st, right?

A Yes.

Q Signed at the station, that was your writing?

A Yes.

Q And then you had her sign it, correct?

A Yes.

Q And you took essentially in addition to that signature, you had another handwriting sample, correct?

[redacted] - Cross

A Yes.

Q And that was on the alcohol influence report, correct?

A Yes.

Q And that was done almost -- maybe a little bit after the second one, correct?

A Yes.

Q The first one was before the breath test and second one was after the breath test, correct?

A Correct.

Q Would you need to take a look at that as well?

MR. INGRASSIA: For the record it's Defendant's A for identification.

Q Would you agree with me that you were able to make out her handwriting there?

A Yes.

Q Take a look at the signature on Defendant's -- I'm sorry, People's 2 in evidence.

A Yes.

Q There is a line there, is there not?

A Uh-huh.

Q And signature looks to be consistently within that line, correct?

A Yes.

[redacted] - Cross

Q Able to make it out, correct?

A Correct.

MR. INGRASSIA: I would just like to step outside with my client. I think I'm just about finished now.

THE COURT: Sure.

(Whereupon, Mr. Ingrassia and the defendant step out of the room.)

MR. INGRASSIA: Nothing further, Your Honor. Thank you, Officer.

THE WITNESS: Yes.

THE COURT: Anything else?

MR. [redacted]: Just a few questions, Judge.

REDIRECT EXAMINATION

BY MR. [redacted]:

Q Officer, on the DWI long form you completed you did not check off the box of impaired motor coordination, did you?

A No, I didn't.

Q And you did fill out other reports relating to the investigation and the field sobriety test that you had the defendant perform that night, correct?

A Correct.

APPENDIX E

SAMPLE TRIAL MEMORANDUM OF LAW

STATE OF NEW YORK : COUNTY OF ORANGE
JUSTICE COURT : TOWN OF
---------------------------------------x
THE PEOPLE OF THE STATE OF NEW YORK

-against-

TRIAL MEMORANDUM OF LAW

Defendant.
---------------------------------------x

The prosecution failed to timely provide discovery of the most recent calibrations of the breath test instrument prior to the defendant's arrest, and as such, the People must be precluded from introducing such evidence.

STATEMENT OF FACTS

The defendant was arrested on by the Town of New Windsor police and charged with two counts of Driving While Intoxicated, respectively in violation of the Vehicle and Traffic Law Sections 1192(2) and 1192(3).

By way of a Demand to Produce dated June 3, 2004, the defendant moved for any and all certificates of calibration for the instrument employed to determine the alcoholic content of the defendant's blood for the preceding year under Paragraph "31". (A copy of the Demand to Produce is attached hereto as **Exhibit A**. In addition, the defendant also moved under paragraph "25" for a copy of the complete maintenance history of the breath test. See **Exhibit A**.

In response to the defendant's Demand to Produce dated June 3, 2004, the People sent in a response on June 8, 2004 as well as on June 30, 2004. Copies of the People's Responses to the defendant's Demand to Produce are attached hereto as **Exhibit B.**

The breath test device that was utilized to determine defendant's blood alcohol level was the Datamaster. Specifically, the serial number was 970075. See State of New York evidence ticket (attached hereto as **Exhibit C**).

THE BREATH TEST RESULT MUST BE PRECLUDED DUE TO THE PEOPLE'S DISCOVERY VIOLATION

An examination of the People's Responses to the defendant's Demand to Produce includes three documents relating to the calibrations and maintenance history of Datamaster Serial No. 970075. (Those specific documents are attached hereto as **Exhibit D**. The first page relating to that document is a certification from John R. Digman, Assistant Director of the Office of Public Safety for the New York State Division of Criminal Justice Services. That certification is made pursuant to CPLR 4518 and maintains the original record of calibration/maintenance of the BAC Datamaster Serial No. 970075 performed on June 5, 2004 by Office of Public Safety employee, Kaylie Lavedure, was made in the regular course of business by the New York State Division of Criminal Justice Services/Office of Public Safety and was made at such time that the calibration was performed or within a reasonable time thereafter. That document is notarized on June 9, 2004. The second page of that document is the Datamaster record calibration. It reflects that the date of calibration was June 5, 2003, and it sets forth various results of the simulator solution that was utilized to calibrate instrument No. 201032. Significantly, that certification is signed by a technician named Kaylie Lavedure and dated January 5, 2003 (see **Exhibit D**).

The last page of the certification record for the calibration/maintenance of instrument No. 970075 establishes what was done to the machine and is dated June 5, 2003 and signed by the technician, Kaylie Lavedure (see **Exhibit D**).

As such, it is clear that the certification page references that calibrations and maintenance were done on June 5, 2003, while the date of the arrest and the defendant's submission to the breath test was on . Therefore, the actual calibration and maintenance record which were provided for the instrument which tested the defendant's breath shows that the machine was calibrated and that repairs were done on June 5, 2003, which is more than 11 months prior to the date of the test. No such calibration or repair records dated within the requisite six month period prior to use of said instrument were provided to defense counsel.

Thus, the defendant objects and moves to preclude the introduction of evidence of any calibrations and maintenance history for instrument No. 970075 as the prosecution has failed to comply with pre-trial discovery by providing the materials that it is obligated to provide under CPL Section 240.20. The prosecution must present all certificates of calibration regarding the breath test machine used to test the defendant's breath in response to a Demand to Produce. Based upon the facts as outlined above and supported by the attached exhibits, the prosecution has failed to provide to the defense the requested documents regarding the defendant's breath test.

As the Court is aware, the prosecution must present proper certificates of calibration in order to lay a proper foundation for the admission of the defendant's breath test. See, People v. Donaldson, 36 AD2d 37 (4th Dept. 1971) (attached hereto as **Exhibit E**). As such, there has been a complete failure for the People to comply with their discovery obligations.

In People v. Corley, 124 AD2d 390 (3rd Dept. 1986) (attached hereto as **Exhibit F**), the Supreme Court Appellate Division reversed the defendant's conviction of two counts of Operating a Motor Vehicle While Under the Influence of Alcohol due to the People's failure to timely turn over discovery of documents relating to the testing and calibration of the breath test device that was used to determine the defendant's blood alcohol level.

In Corley, prior to trial, the defense submitted a Demand to Produce requesting written reports or documents concerning any scientific tests or experiments relating to the criminal action. (In the present case, the defendant made that general demand under Item 2 of his Demand to Produce, attached hereto as **Exhibit A.**) In Corley, the People never produced those documents, and when the defense was supplied the additional documentation at trial, the defendant moved to suppress the test results or alternatively for a continuance. The trial court determined that the Demand to Produce cannot be interpreted as a demand for such documentation, and the trial court denied the motion and the trial ensued resulting in a guilty verdict.

The Appellate Division in Corley reversed the conviction and agreed with the defendant that there was prejudice due to the People's failure to timely produce the documentation as breathalyzer maintenance records amounted to written reports or documents concerning a scientific test relating to the criminal action.

The prosecution's failure to turn over the documents in the Corley case was not found to be harmless error as the admissibility of the breathalyzer test results was contingent upon the prosecution establishing evidence from which the trier fact could reasonably conclude that the breath test device was in proper working order at the time the breath test was administered. See, Corley at 391 citing People v. Freeland, 68 NY2d 699, 700. (A copy of the Freeland decision is attached hereto as **Exhibit G.**)

Based upon the above, the defendant respectfully submits that the failure to turn over the proper calibrations related to instrument No. 970075 during pre-trial discovery precludes the People from being able to introduce the test results upon trial of this matter. See, People v. Corley, 124 AD2d 390; see also, People v. English, 103 AD2d 979 (3rd Dept. 1984) (attached hereto as **Exhibit H),** (holding calibration records of breathalyzer were discoverable and People's failure to turn over such records prior to trial required reversal of two counts of Operating a Motor Vehicle While Under the Influence of Alcohol).

Accordingly, the defendant respectfully objects to the introduction of such calibration and maintenance records and moves to preclude the breath test results attributable to the defendant.

Dated:

Respectfully submitted,

LARKIN, AXELROD, INGRASSIA
& TETENBAUM, L.L.P.
Attorneys for the Defendant
356 Meadow Avenue
Newburgh, New York 12550
(845) 566-5345

APPENDIX F

SAMPLE CROSS-EXAMINATION OF A BREATH TEST OPERATOR

MR. INGRASSIA: Just note my continuing objection, Your Honor.

[redacted] Yes.

A. It was .12.

[redacted] Thank you. I have no further questions.

CROSS-EXAMINATION

BY MR. INGRASSIA:

Q. Good afternoon, Officer [redacted]

A. Good afternoon.

Q. Now, you have been a breath test operator for almost 20 years now; correct?

A. Yes, that's correct.

Q. And that would include being certified on the Smith and Wesson 900A breathalyzer as well as the DataMaster?

A. Yes, sir.

Q. Relative to the operational checklist which was marked as People's Exhibit 5, that's an option K operational checklist for the DataMaster; correct?

A. That's correct.

Q. And you indicated in your direct examination, sir, that every one of those items has to be followed in order to have that test result be

valid; correct?
A. That's correct.
Q. And we can agree that you received your certification from the [redacted] State Department of Health; correct?
A. Yes.
Q. And you were certified as a breath test operator?
A. Yes.
Q. Officer [redacted] you're trained relative to the rules and regulations of the Department of Health; are you not?
A. That's correct.
Q. And you have to take a practical test and a written test to get your certification?
A. Yes.
Q. And we can agree that item number one on that checklist is essentially -- for lack of a better term -- something we call an observation period?
A. Yes, sir.
Q. And that requires -- as does the [redacted] State Department of Health rules -- a continual observation period?
A. That's correct.

Q. And that's where the subject has to be observed, according to the [redacted] Police Department's rules and regulations, continually for 20 minutes; correct?
A. That's correct.
Q. And the Department of Health's requirement is a shorter period of time, but that still requires a 15 minute continuous observation of the subject; correct?
A. Correct.
Q. And we can agree, according to your records -- and if you need to refer to anything, just let me know -- that the actual physical breath sample from my client was obtained by you at 2:32 a.m.; correct?
A. That's correct.
Q. Now, you're positive about that; are you not?
A. Yes.
Q. And we can agree that the start of the observation period that you listed on the operational checklist is 1:48; correct?
A. That's correct.
Q. And the difference between 1:48 a.m. and 2:32 a.m. would be about 44 minutes; correct?
A. Yes, sir.

Q. But we can agree, however, that during that period of time from 1:48 a.m. to 2:32 a.m., you were not continually observing [redacted]; is that a fair statement?

A. Yes, I was continually observing him.

Q. During that entire period of time?

A. Yes.

Q. What time did you place my client under arrest?

A. For that I would have to refer to the sheet.

Q. Is there anything that you could use to refresh your recollection?

A. The bill of particulars.

MR. INGRASSIA: I'd like to have this marked.

(Defendant's Exhibit A, SUPPORTING DEPOSITION BILL OF PARTICULARS 710.30 NOTICE, marked for identification.)

Q. Does looking at that DWI bill of particulars supporting deposition refresh your recollection as to when the defendant was placed under arrest?

A. Yes, at 2:15 a.m.

Q. So at 2:15 a.m., he's physically placed in

handcuffs; correct?
A. That's correct.
Q. And then he's outside of his vehicle and outside of your vehicle when that's done; correct?
A. That's correct.
Q. And we know that after 2:15 a.m. you placed him in your patrol car; correct?
A. That's correct.
Q. And he's in the rear of your vehicle; correct?
A. Correct.
Q. And that's a policy; correct?
A. Yes, sir.
Q. And are you with anybody in your car at that point in time other than my client?
A. No.
Q. So shortly after 2:15, he's in your vehicle; correct?
A. That's correct.
Q. And you're driving?
A. Yes.
Q. And when you're driving, you're looking at the road in front of you; correct?
A. That's correct.
Q. And it takes three minutes -- according to your

testimony, sir -- to get from the arrest location back to the [redacted] Police Department; does it not?
A. That's correct.
Q. So if you leave the arrest location at 2:15, you would get back to the [redacted] Police Department at 2:18; is that correct?
A. That's correct.
Q. And even if it was 2:16 when you left the arrest location, you're still back at the station at 2:19; correct?
A. That's correct.
Q. So let's start with 2:15. Let's assume he's literally placed in the vehicle at 2:15 a.m.; okay?
A. Okay.
Q. And it takes you until 2:18 to get back to the police station; correct?
A. Yes.
Q. And during those three minutes you're not watching [redacted] because you're driving and watching the roadway; correct?
A. Probably in the rearview mirror.
Q. And you have already said, sir, on direct examination that the Department of Health

rules and regulations and the [redacted] Police Department rules and regulations require a continual observation period of 20 minutes for your department and 15 minutes for the New York State Department of Health; correct? [redacted]
A. That's correct.
Q. And you know of no exceptions to that rule; correct?
A. That's correct.
Q. And during the three minutes, according to your own regulations, the department's regulations and the Department of Health's regulations, you were not continually observing him; is that correct?
A. That's correct.
Q. So if it's 2:18 when you arrive back at the police station and the sample is seized at 2:32, that constitutes a 14 minute time difference; correct?
A. Correct.
Q. And we can agree that that 14 minute time difference is less than the time period that the [redacted] State Department of Health rules and regulations mandates you to observe a

subject; correct?

A. Correct.

Q. And it's also less than the 20 minutes that the [redacted] Police Department requires you to continually observe a subject; correct?

A. That's correct.

Q. And there's certain reasons why those requirements are in place; correct?

A. That's correct.

Q. Even if a subject were to have a slight type of belch, that can bring up air from the stomach which could contain alcohol; correct?

A. Correct.

Q. And you never told [redacted] that if he burps or belches that he should report that to you; correct?

A. That's correct.

Q. We can agree, sir, that in your training and experience, you've learned that the device -- in this case, the DataMaster -- is calibrated on a routine basis; correct?

A. That's correct.

Q. And you learned in your training and experience and through your on-the-job experience dealing with breath tests that it's every six months that the machine is sent out for calibrations; correct?

A. That's correct.

Q. We can agree that my client's breath test was performed by yourself on [redacted] correct?

A. Yes, sir.

Q. Now, if you would be kind enough to look at People's Exhibit 2, would you take a moment and look at that, sir?

A. Yes.

Q. That's a calibration relating to this breath test device number [redacted] that was utilized to test [redacted] breath sample; correct?

A. Yes.

Q. And we can agree that that analysis was performed on December 1, 2003; correct?

A. That's correct.

Q. And we can agree that the date of December 1, 2003 is outside of or greater than six months from the date of my client's test of [redacted] 2004; correct?

A. Yes, it's greater.

Q. And you've already told us that in your

training and experience, you know that these breath test devices must be tested every six months; correct?

A. That's correct.

Q. So therefore, that calibration falls outside of that six-month requirement; does it not?

A. Yes, it does.

Q. And you have learned, sir, that that's a requirement for the breath test device to be admitted as accurate and properly functioning; correct?

A. Yes.

Q. Thank you. I appreciate your candor, sir. Now, once you're back at the station, you do have to type in certain informational data relative to the time of the arrest, the age of my client and the name of my client into the keyboard that's attached to the terminal; correct?

A. That's correct.

Q. And during that period of time, where is [redacted] located?

A. He's sitting on the booking room benches.

Q. And where are you located?

A. Standing right across from him.

Q. And the DataMaster is at a little station?
A. It's on the counter.
Q. And as you're typing that information in, are you facing the wall?
A. I'm facing the wall, yes.
Q. And so your back would be to [redacted] correct?
A. That's incorrect; my back would be to the wall behind me, but my face was facing him.
Q. The DataMaster is not up against a wall?
A. It's on a counter.
Q. And you're typing in the information; correct?
A. Yes.
Q. And while you're doing that, you're typing and watching and typing and watching; correct?
A. That's correct.
Q. And the machine gives you a series of prompts letting you know that the machine is ready for the sample; correct?
A. That's correct.
Q. And you ultimately have my client give a breath sample; correct?
A. That's correct.
Q. And you took one sample?
A. Yes.

Q. And that's all the breath test in your department requires; correct?
A. Yes.
Q. We can agree that you're not an expert in the inner workings of the DataMaster and the workings behind it; correct?
A. That's correct.
Q. And you indicated, I believe, that it was an indirect measurement of blood alcohol by measuring the amount of alcohol in his air sample; correct?
A. That's correct.
Q. Did you learn that there are certain assumptions that have to be in place in ratios in order to have that device be reliable?
A. Can you explain that?
Q. Have you ever heard of the blood breath conversion factor that one cc of blood is equivalent to 2,100 millimeters of air?
A. Yes.
Q. And that's something in your training of the breathalyzer that you learned is a constant; correct? In other words, it's average based upon what essentially scientists come up with; correct?

A. Yes.
Q. But you don't know what [redacted] blood breath conversion factor was that evening; correct?
A. I would say that's correct.
Q. So that was an assumption that the machine took into account when it came up with this .12 reading; correct?
A. Yes.
Q. We can also agree that the machine -- that there was a difference of about 44 minutes between the time my client was stopped and operating the vehicle until the actual breath sample; correct?
A. Yes.
Q. And we can agree that there are different stages to the effect of alcohol on the human body once it has actually been ingested; correct?
A. Yes.
Q. You have ingestion?
A. Yes.
Q. And then it goes through your system to your stomach?
A. Yes.

Q. And ultimately it goes to the small intestines and hits the vacular system, and then it goes to the brain and is sent to the central nervous system; correct?
A. Yes.
Q. So there's the ingestion and absorption stages?
A. That's correct.
Q. And ultimately the elimination stage as well?
A. That's correct.
Q. Now, this breath test can only tell us -- assuming it was working properly -- that the subject's breath sample was .12 percent at 2:32 a.m.; correct?
A. That's correct.
Q. And you have no specialized training or experience -- do you, Officer [redacted] -- to testify what my client's blood alcohol content would have been at 1:48 a.m., which was 44 minutes before while he was operating the motor vehicle?
A. I could give you a round figure probably.
Q. But do you have any type of specialized training or certifications in that regard?
A. I do know that the body loses .02 per hour, so you're able to get rid of .02 per hour.

Q. Do you hold any certification in that?
A. That's part of your recertification.
Q. So the only thing you can do is -- assuming that the machine was working 100 percent accurately -- approximate that it would have been perhaps .02 less?
A. That's correct.
Q. Now, turning to the 33.9 centigrade, there's a significance to that; is there not?
A. Yes, sir.
Q. What's the significance of that?
A. Well, it should be 34, but it's okay if it's .1 above or .1 below.
Q. And that's the temperature of the simulator bath; correct?
A. That's correct.
Q. And that simulator solution simulates something; does it not?
A. Yes, it does.
Q. Can you tell the court what it simulates?
A. It simulates -- that's also the same temperature of the breath.
Q. So we can agree then that there's some correlation between the breath of a human who's blowing into a device and the temperature of

that simulator solution; correct?
A. That's correct.
Q. Now, the reason that that temperature is so vital is because if it's less than one-tenth of one degree, it would be no good; is that correct?
A. That's correct.
Q. What was my client's temperature that evening on [redacted]
A. It was 33.9.
Q. That was the reference standard; correct?
A. That's correct.
Q. The reference standard of the simulator solution?
A. Yes.
Q. What was [redacted]s breath temperature on [redacted]
A. I don't test his breath temperature.
Q. Okay. And just so I'm clear and so the court is clear, there's a correlation in order for this device to be reliable that the reference standard of the simulator solution must be within one-tenth of a degree of 34 degrees centigrade, and it's simulating what a subject's actual air breath temperature is;

is that correct?

A. That's correct.

Q. And no air breath temperature of [redacted] was attained that evening; is that correct?

A. That's correct.

Q. So that's another assumption that this machine relied on -- just as it did with the 2,100 to one conversion factor -- in reaching that .12; correct?

A. That's correct.

Q. After you placed my client under arrest at the scene of the arrest, what was done with his vehicle?

A. I would have to recall that.

Q. Did he have a passenger with him?

A. Yes, he did. I think he did.

Q. Was the passenger allowed to drive the vehicle back and meet you at the [redacted] Police Department?

A. I would have to recall that.

Q. Is there anything that would refresh your recollection?

A. Probably the arrest report.

Q. Okay.

A. According to the 710.30 notice, the vehicle was

left there.

MR. INGRASSIA: I'd like to have this marked.

(Defendant's Exhibit B, ARREST REPORT, marked for identification.)

Q. Does looking at that refresh your recollection?
A. Yes, it was turned over to a licensed driver -- the passenger -- at the scene.
Q. And he was allowed to drive home?
A. Yes.
Q. And you had some interaction with that person; correct?
A. That's correct.

MR. INGRASSIA: I have nothing further.

APPENDIX G

SAMPLE CROSS-EXAMINATION FROM A BLOOD TEST CASE

INGRASSIA - CROSS - [redacted]

MS. [redacted]: I believe the court has the original lab report.

THE WITNESS: Is that the original?

MS. [redacted]: Yes. The People would ask that it be moved into evidence as well. No further questions.

MR. INGRASSIA: We already had a lot of testimony by the toxicologist. It's duplicative and he had already testified orally about the results. The Court has obviously taken it subject to the preservation of any objections.

(People's No. 5 marked for identification, this date)

THE COURT: Objection overruled.

CROSS EXAMINATION

BY MR. INGRASSIA:

Q. Mr. [redacted] I represent Mr. [redacted] Just a few questions for you this afternoon. This head space chromatograph you analyzed, did the State Police lab calibrate that?

INGRASSIA - CROSS - [redacted]

A. Yes.

Q. Who was that calibrated by?

A. Myself.

Q. Did you turn over those calibrations to Ms. [redacted]?

A. No, I did not. However on the day of the analysis I ran a series of controls on blanks.

Q. Is that separate and apart from the calibration?

A. Yes.

Q. The calibration does what?

A. It tells us that the instrument is working properly.

MR. INGRASSIA: I would further my objection here on a lot of this testimony and make a demand to produce all the calibrations relating to the device that was utilized to determine the level in the defendant's blood content.

THE COURT: The date of the calibration is what?

THE WITNESS: On the head space chromatograph?

THE COURT: Right.

INGRASSIA - CROSS - [redacted]

THE WITNESS: That was used for this analysis?

THE COURT: To determine Mr. [redacted] blood alcohol content.

THE WITNESS: That was the controls I ran for this particular day. The calibration is done when I prepare those controls.

Q. Just like a breatalyzer, every few months?

A. Yes.

Q. Mr. [redacted], basically everything that you testified -- in other words, you have no personal knowledge as to how these items came into your possession regarding that kit?

A. Up until the time prior to the time it came into the lab, no.

Q. Once you take possession, do you know who touched it or what was done with it before you took possession of it?

A. No.

Q. Once you take possession of it, literally it goes from the vault and you have to sign a form?

A. Yes. The evidence clerk gives me the evidence.

Q. You take it back to your work station then you

INGRASSIA - CROSS - [redacted]

begin your analysis?

A. Correct.

Q. With regard to this analysis of the sample that you've identified to be Mr. [redacted] that's based on what you just read in the submission form, correct? Do you actually analyze his blood alone or is his blood added to other samples at the same time?

A. I analyze one sample, place it in the vial, cap the vial tightly, then I analyze another sample and so on.

Q. Is it in the same column? The column is purged between each analysis?

A. No. The blanks are run along with the samples.

Q. Those blanks are supposed to assure an analyst such as yourself that the column is clear and free of any type of ethanol so cross contamination doesn't take place?

A. Yes.

Q. That, however, would be contingent upon the machine being properly calibrated, would it not?

A. Yes.

Q. The validity of the blank results is done

INGRASSIA - CROSS - [redacted]

separate and apart and is dependant on the machine being in a properly calibrated condition?

A. Yes.

Q. Just so I'm clear, I'm not a chemist or toxicologist, but is it fair to say that you don't actually analyze the liquid volume of blood but rather the vapor or gas above the actual liquid portion, correct?

A. That's correct.

Q. Have you ever heard of anything called hematocritic ratio?

A. Yes. I'm not too familiar.

Q. It's a medical term, correct?

A. Yes.

Q. Do you know what day you analyzed the blood?

A. On November 21.

Q. Do you know what day the blood was drawn?

A. It was submitted to the laboratory on the 20.

Q. You don't know where it was kept between November 18 and the 20?

A. No, I do not.

Q. You don't know what conditions it was kept under until the 20, from November 18

INGRASSIA - CROSS - [redacted]

until November 20, do you?

A. No, I do not.

Q. You did not run any specific independent analysis of those vials you analyzed and testified to the judge about this afternoon regarding any concentration of potassium oxilate or sodium fluoride?

A. It wasn't necessary.

Q. Your purpose was to just determine the contents of ethanol at the lab?

A. Yes.

Q. Do you know what potassium oxilate is?

A. A preservative.

Q. Sodium fluoride?

A. A preservative and anticoagulant.

Q. What is Heparin?

A. I'm not familiar with that.

Q. Have you ever heard of a condition known as neoalcohl fermentation?

A. I might have.

Q. Would there be anything -- when you say you might have, back when you were taking your graduate studies?

A. Maybe I read it.

INGRASSIA - CROSS - [redacted]

Q. How is the blood stored in this container?
A. It was still in the refrigerator.
Q. There is a reason why it needs to be stored in a refrigerator?
A. Yes.
Q. Tell the judge why.
A. To preserve it.
Q. So that it doesn't spoil, correct?
A. Yes.
Q. Do you know that one of the by-products of bacteria could be certainly in the body when extracted from the body?
A. Yes.
Q. Do you know what the by-products are if the blood is not kept in a suitable surrounding?
A. Production of ethanol.
Q. Isn't that the exact item that you were analyzing for?
A. However, the preservative in the tube prevents that from happening.
Q. What preservative is that, potassium oxilate?
A. Yes.
Q. Did you do any analysis sir, on that material in the blood sample that you said was Mr.

INGRASSIA - CROSS - [redacted]

[redacted]'s, for potassium oxilate?

A. No, I did not.

Q. You didn't add anything to that sample, did you?

A. No, I did not.

Q. The reliability of that point one seven result you spoke about is contingent upon the blood being preserved with the proper potassium oxilate, a suitable preservative, and the fact that the device was properly calibrated and there was no contaminants in Mr. [redacted] sample and any in the sample?

A. Yes.

Q. Your point one seven conclusion of your analysis was contingent upon the blood being properly stored during this 48 to 72 hours during which it was in the State Police refrigeration?

A. However, that preservative maintains the integrity for sometime even if it's not refrigerated.

Q. Do you have any personal knowledge of a preservative being present in this vial?

A. No, I do not.

ABOUT THE AUTHORS

John Ingrassia is a partner in the law firm of Larkin, Axelrod, Ingrassia & Tetenbaum LLP, where he practices criminal defense law. Approximately 50 percent of his practice involves defending individuals accused of operating a motor vehicle while under the influence of alcohol. He has successfully defended numerous individuals charged with driving while intoxicated (DWI) offenses at trial, suppression hearings, Department of Motor Vehicle (DMV) hearings, and on appeal. Mr. Ingrassia has served as a lecturer on DWI defense related continuing legal education (CLE) programs given to other attorneys on behalf of the New York State Bar Association as well as local bar associations. In addition, he has been a guest speaker on behalf of the New York State Office of Court Administration training judges on DWI related issues. He is also a former prosecutor.

Mr. Ingrassia is an accomplished appellate attorney having successfully argued appeals in a variety of appellate courts in this state including the New York State Court of Appeals.

Mr. Ingrassia graduated with honors from Saint Bonaventure University and graduated with honors from Syracuse University College of Law.

He is admitted to practice law in New York State as well as the United States District Court for the Southern District of New York.

Kathleen V. Wells is an associate of the law firm Larkin, Axelrod, Ingrassia & Tetenbaum LLP. Since graduating from law school, she has primarily focused her attention on criminal law and the representation of clients charged with DWI and related offenses. Ms. Wells has spoken throughout the state at continuing legal education seminars about DWI law and jury selection. She has successfully defended DWI clients at trial, pre-trial hearings, DMV administrative hearings, and on appeal. She currently has a DWI case pending before New York State's highest court, the Court of Appeals. Ms. Wells is a graduate of Thomas More College of Liberal Arts and Albany Law School.

ASPATORE